Beau

Ball Gowns

The Best of Crown of Beauty Magazine!

Written by

Livy Jarmusch, Deanna Bridges, Tiffany Dawn, Hailey Gardiner, Alyssa Gibbs, Kenya-Nicole Gossett, Noelle Hilpert, Natalee Jensen, Nellie Martin, Melody Mohnhaupt, Lorna Penn, Natasha Sapienza, and Hannah Wilson.

Cover Credits: LaRue Photography
{www.facebook.com/JessicaLaRuePhotography}
Company: Verity Vareé
www.facebook.com/verityvaree
www.verityvaree.com

ISBN-13: 978-1517360658

Table of Contents...
Part 1: Beauty

PART 1: BEAUTY

A Letter From Livy

I grew up reading *American Girl* Magazine. I devoured each issue and dreamed of the day I could create my own magazine. I wrote movie reviews, advice articles, and created quizzes and sent them to my friends in the mail. My passion was to write, so write I did!

As I grew out of *American Girl* and into my teenager years, I was still drawn to magazines. The glossy covers and bright-colored headlines beckoned me to take a peek inside. I would read about my favorite stars, take quizzes that told me whether or not I would make a good girlfriend for Nick Jonas, and I drooled over the celebrity lifestyle I read about.

As a homeschooled girl living in Michigan, my life was far from the glam of Hollywood. I wasn't movie star gorgeous, wasn't the star of the local school musical, and didn't have a boyfriend who looked like Zac Efron. I found myself growing painfully dissatisfied with who I was and where I was headed.

I could never be the charismatic blonde who lit up every beach party with her sassy charm. I wasn't doll-faced Taylor Swift who could have any guy she wanted by tossing her flawless hair over her shoulders and throwing a flirtatious look across the room. I didn't have a thousand friends on Facebook.

According to Hollywood and the standards of this world, I was quite pathetic.

What I was reading in these teen magazines told me how to snatch the perfect boyfriend, be popular, become famous and look stunning. Yet, none of this was happening for me.
And the more I read these *MUST*-do articles, the more I felt I didn't measure up.

My generation has been forced to conform to impossible standards. We've been told that our beauty and self-worth lies in our closet, our dress size, how many friends or Twitter followers we have, what kind of car we drive, how cute our boyfriend is, or how successful we are.

Believing these things to be true is devastating. These lies can push you into a lowly place on the ground, and cram you into a cycle of depression and dissatisfaction. Trying to get back up after feeling so defeated is like someone has a foot pressed on your stomach. It's hard to stand up again. This generation of girls has been forced to crawl around on the ground for too long...we've been asked to stoop down to disgustingly low standards.

Princess, It's Time To Awaken
Like a world full of real life Sleeping Beauties we've touched worldly spindles out of curiosity and rebellion, and it's placed us in a deep and fitful sleep. At age fourteen, my heart was awakened with a kiss. Not by any man, but rather the Creator and Lover of my soul.

He rubbed the sleep out of my eyes, told me to get out of my apathetic nightgown, took me to the high places of His Kingdom, and showed me something spectacular.

He bestowed a crown of beauty upon me, dressed me in breathtakingly-beautiful garments of salvation, transformed my mind, and called me a Princess.

Princess. My royal identity redefined who I am. No longer am I forced to crawl around in the mud desperately trying to conform to what I found inside magazine pages. I am free to live extravagantly and without insecurity!

And so are you.

How do I know this?

Because you're a Princess too.

You might not live in a royal palace, wear a physical crown on your head, or waltz around school wearing big fluffy ball gowns.

But if you've crowned Jesus Christ as Lord of your life then His royal blood has become yours! Your royal identity is forever established in Heaven. The only question now is, are you going to believe it?

Will you shake off those lies of darkness that have tormented you for so long and step into the brilliant light of your identity in Him?

The purpose of this magazine is to help you do just that!

Crown of Beauty's Mission is to:
-Proclaim good news of freedom to His captive daughters of all ages.

-Awaken the Sleeping Beauties.

-Remind you of what Christ has already done for you, and that as an heir, you no longer have to live like a slave.

-Comfort the broken hearts.

-Remind you that you're not alone.

-Remind you that you are a crown of beauty in God's hand and are being daily transformed by His splendor! {Check out Isaiah 62:3}

-Encourage you to become the best YOU that you can be for His glory.

-Remind you how radically loved you are.

-And that you are crazy beautiful.

And perhaps most importantly, this magazine is here to say that you *DON'T* have to conform to the exhausting patterns of this world. {Romans 12:2}

I believe that this generation of girls can totally change our world. Maybe I'm crazy, but I suppose I am brainwashed. I've listened to "One Girl Revolution" by *Superchic[K]* one too many times. I've drowned my mind in the truth of God's Word, and it has filled me with faith! I believe that we are called to be world changers!

I believe the words of Paul in Romans 12:2, which explain how this works. If I refuse to conform to this world, and instead allow myself to be transformed by His Word and His Grace, then I will test and approve His good, pleasing, and perfect will. Whoa, doesn't that make you excited? What could God's good, pleasing, and perfect will for our lives possibly look like? I am going to make it my mission to find out! To answer the *What if's* that are floating around in my mind.

What if we were a generation of young women who understood our royal role in His Kingdom? *What if* we didn't struggle with fear, insecurity, and feeling un-beautiful? *What if* we were a generation on fire, totally in love with King Jesus?

The Biblical prophet, Habakkuk, spoke about the days we are living in:

"Look at the nations and watch - and be utterly amazed. For I am going to do something in your days that you would not believe, even if you were told."
Habakkuk 1:5

Sisters, we live in a most exciting time in history. The Lord is writing a beautiful story, and wants us to take part in it! Will you be a Daughter who asks, *What if? What if* I immerse myself in God's presence and His Word and allow Him to change the way I think about myself? *What if* I surrender all to Him, and light this world on fire? Hmm...*what if?*

Crown of Beauty Magazine is encouragement for all Jesus-loving, anti-conforming, *ONE GIRL REVOLUTION*ists! It's for all my Princess sisters and future world changers. So yes, that would be you, missy!

~Livy Lynn, Founder of *Crown of Beauty Magazine*

~*~

About the Author:
21-year-old Livy Jarmusch is a dreamer, singer, songwriter, and orphan advocate. As the founder of *Crown of Beauty*, she strives to reach young girls and inspire them to realize their true worth in Christ.

She loves fairy-tales, the smell just after it rains, golden retriever puppies and peppermint ice-cream cones. If you really want to get to know her, follow her on Pinterest, and if you find yourself repinning everything, you're sure to be the best of friends! To join this princess on her pilgrimage through life, follow on instagram @livylynnglittergirl & Pinterest @livyglittergirl

She is currently raising funds to build an orphanage in India for precious princess sisters and future world changers. To donate or find out how you can get involved, visit missions.me/crownofbeautyorphanage

Beautiful Lies

Imagine. You're in the middle of math class, attempting to unscramble a page of foreign numbers and odd-ball letters. (Seriously, who invited the alphabet to join algebra?) Your cell phone quietly vibrates in your pocket. You glance up at the teacher then reach for it when you're confident she's not looking. A secret code is depicted on your screen. You know what it means. As a top-secret federal agent, you're familiar with the red alert code. Your latest assignment is to eavesdrop on a boardroom full of dark terrorists who desire to take over the world.

You raise your hand and request a hall pass and a bathroom break. Your teacher is hesitant, but hands it to you anyway...some of the other girls giggle. They're growing suspicious of your frequent quick exits...it's like you have to go the bathroom WAY too often. As soon as you enter the school yard, you let your boss know you're free to work, and a long black limousine picks you up.

Your homework will have to wait 'til tomorrow. Trivial, daily thoughts of what you'll be eating for lunch and if your crush will notice you're gone in science lab are replaced with weightier thoughts. You begin to pray and steady your heart. It's time to get serious. After arriving at the mission ground in a tall, New York City skyscraper, you slip into a cloak of invisibility and enter the boardroom unseen. You're about to get all the top-secret information.

You see a screen hanging on the wall, where an image of your little sister pops up. You try to catch your breath as your heart freezes. Your sister is the target of their evil plans! A whole new fiery passion revs up inside you. How dare they mess with your sister! As their secret scheme unravels, you learn that this image is a hologram from the future. It's a video of your sister ten years down the road, throwing up in the bathroom, starving herself to feel beautiful.

You blink, dumbfounded, as you stare at the video. How can this be real? What kind of wicked plan could be powerful enough to convince your bright-blue-eyed, charismatic, lovable sis to feel ugly?

On the video screen, your little sister is soon joined by your best friend.

Next, you see the daughter of your youth pastor, your childhood friend from Kindergarten, and the captain of your soccer team.

Your invisible self nearly slips off your chair; you've leaned in so close to the frightening scene. You're beyond shocked. What's going to happen next in this holographic image from the future? What are these evil men planning? You watch the video frantically, as the long line of beautiful girls are led into a dark room and are ordered to stand against a wall. Men with guns enter and aim.

You can't believe this! The bad guys have targeted your little sister, your best friends, and every girl you've ever met. They desire to assassinate and demolish all these ladies! A righteous anger rises up inside you. How dare these guys try to mess with your sisters!

~*~

Okay, it's back to reality. What was that all about? Dare to linger a few moments longer in that frightening fantasy and I will explain. But first, a question for you:

If the spy scene above actually happened to you, what would you do *today* to keep that vision from coming true *tomorrow*? Would you call your boss right away and ask what needs to be done? Would you kill the men who sabotaged your friends' hearts and lives? Would you tell the ladies in your life how much you love them, and remind them every day how gorgeous they are?

Don't leave the boardroom just yet. Return once more and you will see...

You're crazy mad, and ready to do what needs to be done. Another face pops up on the screen. You can't believe it. The face of the girl you see now is the girl you see every day in the mirror. There is an attack on every girl of this generation. Including *you.*

Unless you've been living in a cave for the past fifteen years of your life, or dwell on an Amish farm out in the hilly countryside, you've probably noticed the way in which the media has a special gift for making girls feel ugly and inadequate. We've all suffered through those nauseating T.V. advertisements in which an underwear model poses, pursing her pouty lips, as her hair blows wildly from a fan. After watching such ads, I roll my eyes and try not to laugh. I mean, how lame do the marketers think I am?! (It's like those drug advertisements that list the deadly side effects, such as hearing loss or your nose falling off, while they show happy old couples flying kites and walking puppy dogs.)

I'm sure you've picked up on the trend in many teen magazines. The words on the glossy cover shout, "Boost Your Self-Confidence! Six Tips To Loving Yourself!" Yet by the time you flip to page ten, you've already seen a dozen perfect faces and bodies posing for makeup advertisements, which drained away all confidence you were hoping to get from their pep-talk article. Every girl has noticed what's going on. We're not immune to it. But have we ever recognized what's going on around us as a *targeted attack* on our beauty as females?

The opening scene in this article, where you imagined yourself to be a top-secret agent exposing a hidden scheme, isn't a fantasy action tale. It's a reality. This deadly terror attack isn't coming from the media or the makeup marketers. Even though they profit greatly from our beauty insecurities, they didn't create this problem.

The sickening plot has been dreamt up and skillfully executed by the enemy of our souls, Satan. He has always hated girls. Ever since the Garden of Eden, he has been attacking Eve and all her daughters with lies that spew like fire out of his dragon mouth.

The purpose of this disgusting scheme is to convince God's chosen daughters that they are worthless. The familiar scenery of the hour we live in, the set on this stage, and the cast of characters in this story remind me of what unfolded in Esther's day. Esther's story is a dramatic tale that all of us love. An ordinary, average, orphan girl was called to play a magnificent role in the Kingdom, and God used her to release her entire generation from destruction. Just like Esther you were called into the kingdom for *such a time as this*.

Girl, your adrenaline-pumping, high-action story of greatness is unfolding. You are living in the midst of this BEAUTY-saturated generation for a purpose, and that purpose is not to remain silent and be destroyed. There is no need for fear because we know how this story ends. The victory is not in jeopardy; it already belongs to Christ. He is calling you to walk with Him into this adventure.

Girl Meets World...Girl Meets God

In order to know what our battle plan of attack should be, we need to find out where this all started. Let's step into a Time Machine and zip back through the ages...all the way to the Garden of Eden. This is where the first woman believed a lie. This lie did not pertain to beauty, but it did promise a certain element of greatness. Satan said, "Eat this forbidden fruit, and you will be like God!"

What Eve did not remember or failed to embrace is that she was *already* made in God's image. Why would she reach out for something that she already had? We must ask ourselves, why did Eve eat from that tree? Because she thought God was holding something back from her. Eve believed there was something GOOD or BETTER that she couldn't have, that God had robbed her of.

And isn't the story the same for us? We strive to enhance our natural beauty and chase things that will help us feel better about ourselves because we don't realize who we already are. The enemy's tactic today is simple but powerful. It worked with Eve, and so the Liar continues his crafty skill to this very day. He tries to get us focused on everything we DON'T have. He shows us images of cute boys, pretty hair, dazzling bags, flawless faces, flashy cars, glamorous lifestyles, and skinny models. Then he says, "You really should have this. You really need to be this. You really should chase this. Why didn't God give you this? Look how ugly you are compared to her. He doesn't really love you as much as you think He does, because He has denied you the pleasure of a good gift."

James 1:16-17 says, "Don't be deceived, my dear brothers and sisters. Every good and perfect gift is from above, coming down from the Father of the heavenly lights, who does not change like shifting shadows."

To be deceived is to see God in a distorted form. When thoughts of God enter your mind, do you imagine He is holding something back from you? Or do you see Him standing before you with arms wide open? The root of all deception comes from not believing that God has and IS every good and perfect gift...and that He desires to give all good things (which is Himself!) to us. There is truly nothing good for us outside the will of God. When the Lord asks us to trade in one of our selfish ways for His perfect ways, we always get the better end of the deal. Everything He asks us to do is for our own good! The enemy does not want us to believe that, so he never ceases to lie about who God is and who we are as His daughters.

Just like Cinderella's evil step-mother, the enemy is jealous of our potential and royal position. He knows we are stunning and splendorous...so he tries his very best to lie to us and convince us that we are not. He says we are worthless, powerless, ugly and unloved. But he knows the truth...and it frightens him. We are priceless, powerful, beautiful, and radically loved! Imagine what damage an army of girls, who understand who they are in Jesus and walk in their royal identity, could do to the enemy's plans!

If we don't know or believe the truth, we offer no threat to him. But once we grasp and understand this truth...we become unstoppable! The enemy tries to keep us from our Cinderella-style, God-given destiny that is more exciting and exhilarating than we could dream. He would like us to continue gazing into the mirror, despising, comparing, and hating ourselves...

Why does he work so tirelessly to discourage us as young women? I believe the enemy hates us so intensely for two reasons.

1) He is Jealous of Our Beauty
This sounds like a wild thought, but it's a Biblical one. Ezekiel 28:12 describes the enemy in this way; "You were the signet of perfection, full of wisdom and perfect in beauty."

Lucifer (also known as Satan, or the devil) was a handsome, attractive angel. 2 Corinthians 11:14 says he disguises himself as an angel of light. God said he was perfect in beauty! But apparently Lucifer enjoyed looking at himself in the mirror. He became obsessed with himself. But God couldn't stand to be around pride. "Your heart was proud because of your beauty; you corrupted your wisdom for the sake of your splendor." (Ezekiel 28:17) Jesus said that Lucifer's bad attitude got him kicked out of Heaven. (Luke 10:18).

Only Satan himself knows just how much his puffed up arrogance and selfishness cost him. And now, aware of how short his time is on earth before he is cast away to eternal torment in the Lake of Fire (Revelation

20:10) his evil goal is to drag everyone he possibly can down with him. Even though he cannot shake our eternal security of being Heaven-bound (as long as we are following Christ), Satan attempts to discourage us in every way possible with such a great wrath, hatred and jealousy. He knows what a slippery slope it is for God's beautiful ones to become obsessed with ourselves and worship our own images. The Deceiver is really good at his job, which only makes it all the more important that we know the truth! I apologize if I'm getting a little heavy here with talk about Satan, and Hell, and how much he hates us.

But girls, we've got to see what's happening in the hour we're living in. Not so that we will be discouraged and depressed by the darkness - but rather that we will look to Christ and partner with our Mighty Warrior and Conquering Savior! He has commissioned us to sparkle and illuminate the darkness with the light He has placed inside us. We can't do that if we aren't aware of what's going on!

2) He is Afraid of Us

In Exodus, Chapter 1, Pharaoh started to oppress the Israelites and made them his slaves because he was afraid of them. Verse 12-13 says, "But the more they were oppressed, the more they multiplied and spread; so the Egyptians came to dread the Israelites and worked them ruthlessly."

The same is true of our enemy. The more he attempts to oppress us in fear and dread, the more we rise up and turn to Christ! The enemy cannot win, but he is desperately giving his best fight. But we must determine to keep our eyes fixed on eternity, the happily ever after, and refuse to agree with his cunning lies. He chooses to target the girls because we have a very strong influence over the men in our lives. Remember who followed Eve's lead, after she ate the forbidden fruit? It was Adam! If the enemy can rip down the princesses, he can successfully keep the men from fulfilling their royal roles as well.

For Such a Time as This

We have just learned a lot of new information. We are now responsible for what we know. We cannot allow things to be the way they've always been. With this knowledge, we can't sit back, sip on a Pepsi and say, "Those poor girls who struggle fighting off lies. I hope they get better soon," then go on our merry way. If you're a Christian, you've been called to proclaim liberty to the captives and bestow beauty on those who feel like their lives are in ashes (Isaiah 61).

If you don't struggle to appreciate your beauty and self-worth, and are confident in your identity in Christ, that's awesome sister! You may feel like some of this does not apply to you, or perhaps you have never struggled in this way. But I can pretty much guarantee that there is a girl in your life right now who needs you to share what you've learned. She needs to know the truth about who she is in Christ, and why she doesn't have to listen to lies anymore!

Just like Queen Esther, every girl has been given a sphere of influence, a place where she can make a difference. We've each been planted in a garden, where we live and grow, and touch the lives of many others. God desires that our lives be like an Eden, a place where He can touch others with His life and His love flowing out of us. As keepers of our own gardens, we must be careful and watch out for deception. We also need to look and see who is hanging out in our garden. Who can we protect and care for in prayer and love? Who can we influence? For some girls, their garden of influence is at church, school, around their friends, the little kids they babysit, or the blog they update. Whoever you are, I can promise that you have people you interact with every day that are powerfully influenced by you.

As a guard in my own garden, I will not sit around and watch the enemy deceive and destroy my sisters. I cannot remain silent about his twisted plot. It's the prayer of my heart that the passion etched into these pages will ignite a flame in your innermost being. I encourage you to pray as you read this, and every article in the magazine. Let God's Holy Spirit gently blow on your soul and increase that ember glow that's twinkling inside you. May it result in a dangerous wildfire as we declare war against the enemy.

Let passion and protection for your sisters reign in YOUR garden.

~*~

QUIZ! Just How Beauty Obsessed Are You?

Are you obsessed with your appearance? Or do you have a healthy attitude about the girl in the mirror? Take this quiz to find out! Read through the questions and circle each letter that applies. Tally up your letters at the end to discover your beauty-obsession status!

1. You wake up, look at your alarm clock, and *gasp* you realize you only have 10 minutes until you have to leave for school! What do you do beauty-wise before you leave?

A. Psh, personal hygiene? Ain't nobody got time fo dat! Skip the toothpaste and deodorant. I'll spray myself with air freshener before I run out the door.

B. Run a comb through my hair and brush my teeth. Just the essentials. Nothing but all-natural beauty today.

C. The essentials + a little mascara and lip gloss. Nothing major!

D. I would rather be late for class than show up bare-faced, so I slap on as much makeup as I can and then finish the rest in the car.

2. How long does it usually take you to get ready?

A. It takes me about 27 seconds to run a hose over my head. If I'm feeling extra spiffy, I might chew some tic-tacs to ward off bad breath.

B. Maybe about 15 minutes to shower, get dressed, etc.

C. Anywhere from 20 - 45 minutes. I usually wear a little makeup, but nothing too time consuming.

D. If I could take all day, I would! Curling my hair, perfecting my eyeliner, and picking out the perfect body spray takes me well over an hour.

3. How many times have you dyed your hair?

A. Pretty sure it used be to blonde back in the day, but all the dirt build-up changed it to a lovely mud-brown color. So I guess you could say I dyed it once.

B. Never, and I don't really plan on it.

C. Once or twice, and I might again in the future. Not really sure.

D. More than three times. I love changing it up.

4. You've been stranded on a desert island for 15 long, lonely years. When you finally get discovered, your discoverers bring a TV crew with them. They want to interview you right away! What do you say?

A. Noooooo! Leave me alone! I want to stay here with my baboon friends!

B. Step right up, camera crew! Boy, do I have a story for YOU!

C. At least let me take a shower first. I mean, it HAS been 15 years!

D. Um, where's my makeup artist!? This sunburn ain't gonna cover itself!

5. What's your usual reaction when flipping through a teen magazine?

A. The only thing I would use a teen magazine for is toilet paper.

B. I'm not usually interested. It all seems sort of fake to me.

C. I find some of the articles interesting, but not all of them.

D. To be honest, I get really jealous when I see all the models with perfect skin and bodies.

6. If you searched your purse right now, what would you most likely find?

A. An old baloney sandwich, a frog, and part of my lint collection.

B. I don't normally carry a purse.

C. My wallet, keys, maybe some Chapstick. That sort of thing.

D. Pretty much my complete makeup collection. You never know when you're gonna need to touch up something!

7. If you had a gift card to a beauty supply store, what would you most likely buy?

A. Absolutely nothing! I avoid those places like the plague!

B. Maybe some bath products or lotion.

C. A cute shade of lip gloss or that new BB cream I've been wanting to try!

D. How in the world could I possibly choose!? It would be a hard decision because I want almost everything!

8. You have a date tonight with the one and only ____ (insert name of current celebrity crush. May I suggest Zac Efron?) What do you do to prepare for the big event?

A. Lock myself in my room and scream like a banshee. I don't do dates.

B. Take a shower and brush those pearly whites. Nothing fancy here.

C. Apply some makeup and do my hair. I'll try to look nice, of course, but nothing that I wouldn't normally do.

D. I'll hire a professional makeup artist to transform me into absolute perfection. Oh, and I'll bring a personal assistant along to make sure I don't lose a false eyelash during our date.

9. How confident do you feel going completely all natural? (No makeup or hair products?)

A. Considering I don't even own a single bar of soap, I would say pretty confident.

B. Extremely confident! I don't ever use anything anyway.

C. Fairly confident. I never wear anything too heavy, so it wouldn't be that big of a difference.

D. Not very confident at all. Makeup makes me feel a lot more beautiful than I feel without it.

10. What's your current fingernail state?

A. Last time I counted, I still have all 10.

B. Healthy and shiny, but no polish.

C. They're painted my favorite color, of course!

D. I'm wearing super cute fake nails.

TALLY UP YOUR SCORE & FLIP THE PAGE!

IF YOU GOT MOSTLY A's...

Well, you aren't hung up on beauty, that's for sure. Just remember that a little personal hygiene never hurt anyone. It's okay to take a shower and pick the bugs out of your hair every once in a while.

IF YOU GOT MOSTLY B's...

You're a very down-to-earth, low-maintenance kinda girl. And there's nothing wrong with that! Feeling confident in your own skin is awesome, and if makeup isn't your thing, then that's a-okay. Rock what you got!

IF YOU GOT MOSTLY C's...

You like to dabble in a little bit of the beauty world, but you don't let it consume you. That's great! There's nothing wrong with enjoying makeup and cute hairstyles as long as you find a good balance.

IF YOU GOT MOSTLY D's...

You looove beauty products! Your motto is probably the more glamour, the better. Although there's absolutely nothing wrong with enjoying makeup, just remember that you are truly beautiful without any concealer, mascara, or fancy shampoo. You don't need any of those things to be the gorgeous, treasured girl that God made you to be.

~*~

What Makes a Girl Beautiful?

I believe that beauty is more than hair color, the clothes you wear, the products you use, and your body type. I believe that beauty is in the eye of the beholder, and I often wonder why we feel the need to compare ourselves to the unrealistic and superficial standards of beauty, set by people who seem to constantly make us feel like we'll never measure up. In a world of mass media marketing, we are constantly bombarded with photos, commercials, and articles attempting to convince us that if we wear a certain brand of mascara, we'll have long, full eyelashes; if we buy this pair of jeans, we'll be confident enough to talk to the cute guy who sits across from us in Chemistry; if we have perfect hair and skin like the actresses on the red carpet, we'll be happy.

Would we *really* be happy?

When I was in eighth grade, I moved from a laid back town where people spent a lot of time outdoors, to a school across the country where girls my age cared more about their outfits and hair than they did about their grades.

We're not in Kansas anymore, Toto.

I started saving up my 13-year-old allowance money to buy similar, name-brand clothes and shoes, to be like the pretty and popular girls in my grade. I thought if I wore makeup, had a monogrammed backpack and rocked Sperry boaters, I would be accepted, make lots of friends, and get the attention of the boys I liked. Amidst this shift to a new school and life, what was supposed to be a doctor's check-up ended up changing my limited perspective and ultimately my lifestyle forever.

Near the middle of my 8th grade year, I was diagnosed with severe idiopathic Scoliosis. Scoliosis is the abnormal curvature of the spine, which most often appears in pubescent-aged girls and sometimes boys, and gradually worsens over time. My curvature was severe enough to require aggressive treatment, but thankfully I was not far enough along to need the standard, highly invasive spinal surgery often required to straighten the spine. As an attempt to inhibit the worsening curve of my spine, I was given a full torso prosthetic brace to wear for 23 hours-a-day, 7 days-a-week, until my body was done growing. I was allowed to take the brace off to shower and for my ballet classes, but aside from that I walked, sat, slept, ran, and lived my life in that brace. I was devastated. I was convinced that no one would want to be friends with a girl who wore plastic armor under her clothes. I remember attending my ballet class the night I was told about the brace, and staring at the other girls whose perfectly straight spines and strong ballerina backs I had never noticed before. I noticed because I believed that "beautiful" girls didn't have crooked spines.

For the next two years, I lived my life in my brace, and it became a part of me. I acquired a new wardrobe of clothes two sizes too big, to fit over the brace, and learned how to adapt in it. I had to creatively pick up things I'd dropped on the floor, learn to sleep comfortably without moving, learn how to do sit-ups in gym, and deal with the intense North Carolina summer heat in a stifling hot prosthetic. Every day was a personal victory for me as I grew to know I was loved and cared about, even though I looked different from girls my age. In a time when I could have retreated and lost all confidence in myself, I chose to face my fear of being a social outcast, with a determination not to let my condition hold me back. I continued to dance and even joined the swim team my freshman year of High School. I began practicing yoga and became more flexible, aware, and at peace with my body. I faithfully wore the brace and saw many doctors and specialists, who helped me find alternative options to surgery and taught me how to manage my condition. Although it was uncomfortable, awkward, bulky, and at times painful, my brace was critical in helping me discover and sharpen my identity during those years. I became confident in the aspects of my body and character that were within my control, and quickly realized that no one treated me differently because of my Scoliosis. My friends even named the brace, and would punch my "rock solid" stomach as a greeting, often stunning strangers who would hear the loud WHACK their fists made upon contact.

When my doctors felt that I was nearly done growing, it came time for me to ease out of the brace. I remember feeling strange without the support it offered my body, and my post-brace x-rays showed that my curvature had slightly improved over the course of my treatment. With the help of my family and friends, I had overcome what I thought was impossible. I knew then, that I was so much more than my body. My spine is not who I am, it's just a part of what makes me, me!

Since my time in the brace, my battle with my continually worsening Scoliosis is something I still deal with every single day. Even though it is obvious to me that my spine is crooked, my ribs stick out, one leg is longer than the other, and I can't sit or stand for long periods of time, nobody else EVER notices. I know that those little things make me who I am, but they are not everything I am. When others look at me they might initially see what's on the outside, but what I want them to see is that I know I'm beautiful the way I am. I know that God loves me, and that he has given me a perfectly imperfect body so I can understand what it's like to be different, to be lonely, and to not feel beautiful sometimes.

I believe that true beauty is something that can't be bought; it's something that can't be tanned, dressed up, powdered, faked, baked, or photoshopped. True beauty has more to do with a girl's realization of her inner potential and the strength of her character. A beautiful girl exudes confidence, happiness, kindness, and love. She is thoughtful and respectful of others. She understands that her decisions impact not only the course her life will take, but also affects the people surrounding her. She is determined and hardworking, and continues working when others would give up. She's the first to show up to help and the last to leave, the girl who makes friends with those who may be lonely or new. She's the kind of girl who isn't afraid to stand up for what she knows is right, even if everyone else is doing it.

A beautiful girl knows that she is not her body, and chooses to love the little imperfections that make her who she is.

Believe you are beautiful, not the way the world wants you to be, but the kind of beautiful that surpasses trends, age, and culture. True beauty is the kind of beauty that shines through over-sized clothes, crooked spines, and a prosthetic back brace.
I believe it. Do you?

~*~

About the Author:
Hailey Gardiner is the eldest sister of YouTube sensations, The Gardiner Sisters. Their spunky and spirited cover of a One Direction song has gotten over 4 million views!
Hailey strives to encourage her little sisters and all their fans to be a bright light of goodness and joy in the world.
Visit their blissfully fun YouTube channel: youtube.com/GardinerSisters

I Survived the Pinterest Apocalypse

The shocking story of a young girl who nearly lost her sanity to the wonderful world of pinning. Read with caution. This account may encourage sudden urges to pin! If you are a recovering Pinterest addict, please seek professional counsel before proceeding.

"Have you ever heard of Pinterest?" Six small and seemingly innocent words. Who knew that they could have such a dangerous impact on my life? Who knew that once those words were spoken, my life would change forever? I would go from being a happy, busy, socializing person to...this.

But I suppose I should start from the beginning. It all started a couple of years ago. The tragedy began on a cool day in mid-October. It was that perfect time of year where it's just cold enough for a jacket, but still warm enough to be outside without having to worry about icicles growing on your nose. In other words: perfect bonfire weather. And that's just where I happened be that night. The exact details are a blur, but one moment stands clear in my mind. I was standing in a group, innocent and unknowing of what was to come. We were laughing and having a grand ole time, when that life-altering phrase was spoken. "Have you ever heard of Pinterest!?" my friend Winifred suddenly asked (her name has been changed to protect her identity, of course).

"No, what is it?" I replied, curious.

"It's basically like an online bulletin board where you pin your favorite stuff. Sounds weird, I know, but it's awesome. Want me to send you an invite?" It did sound weird, and I didn't really think I would like it, but I figured "sure, why not?" Winifred promised to send me an email invite later on, and the conversation was soon changed. Little did I know the danger that loomed ahead. A few uneventful days passed before I decided to check my email.

Sitting there amongst spam mail promising to find me my soulmate, something caught my eye: "You've Been Invited To Join Pinterest!" If only lightning would've struck my computer at that moment. If only a swarm of angry beavers would've broken into my room and carried away my computer. If only Marty McFly would've poofed in from the future and warned me of my oncoming fate. Sadly, none of those things happened.

Instead, I clicked on the link and was instantly transported into another dimension known as...Pinterest. I was dazzled. Mystified. Enchanted. Before my eyes swam dozens of pictures, all of them even more impressive than the one before it. Did I die and go to heaven!? I wondered as I scrolled slowly down the page, taking in every detail with wide eyes and an open mouth. Gazillion-jillion-dollar wedding dresses, intricate crafts made from toilet paper tubes, and triple-layer-calorie-laden desserts. Perfectly-put-together outfits, tutorials on how to do your hair in less than 17 seconds, and a whole board dedicated to Liam Hemsworth. Cat pictures galore and perfect makeup. "I'm finally home," I managed to say as a single tear of joy made its way down my cheek. I felt as if my whole life was sitting in front of me now, ready for me to plan and organize and dream. And that's exactly what I did. Minutes passed like seconds. Hours passed like minutes. Before I knew it, I had planned not only every detail of my imaginary wedding, but I also had planned the honeymoon, the house we would move into, and every meal I would make for the first 50 years of our marriage. The only thing missing in my future life was my husband.

Somewhere in those first few hours of my Pinning madness, my Mom had tried to save me. "Alyssa, are you gonna come eat dinner?" she asked, eying me with a look of concern in her eyes.

"Just leave some food out for me, I'll be fine," I managed to say, clicking furiously. "I just need to pin a few more outfits." 'A few more outfits' wasn't quite accurate. The deeper I got into Pinterest, the more work I discovered I needed to do. Some girl in Brazil had a board dedicated to her pet iguana's wardrobe, which meant that I needed one too. Never mind that I didn't even own an iguana. I was sure I would someday. After all, one of the house designs I had pinned had a room on the 4th story, which would be just perfect for my little reptilian friend.

Days began to pass so quickly that I scarcely had time to wave at them as they went by. Sleep? Who needs it? Food? Pshh. I have 367 boards full of delicious recipes, and looking at them is more than enough. Who cares that I haven't showered within the past 2 weeks. I have a recipe for homemade shampoo that only requires salt, Kool-Aid and the tears of a young alpaca! How many years did I spend trapped in the arms of Pinterest? Only the Lord knows. Eventually, woodland animals made nests in my hair. I didn't mind the company, because my family had long since given up hope on me. Could I blame them? Of course not. To be honest, I scarcely remembered who they were. Pinterest was my family now. Pinterest was my mother, father, siblings, and obnoxious uncle. It was my life.

And then...it happened. Call it whatever you want, but I stand firm in my belief that it was divine intervention. Flashes and sparks erupted in front of my eyes, sending me flying backwards in a panicked frenzied. I could only watch in horror as my computer finally exploded into a pile of smoldering ashes, no doubt brought on by years of too much mouse-clicking. I could scarcely believe it. Shock and despair covered me like a wet blanket. I wailed so loudly that the chipmunk family living in my hair got up and fled the premises immediately. I'm really not sure how long I mourned the loss of all my plans and dreams, but when I finally opened my tear-stained eyes, I noticed the sun was shining outside. Aah...the sun. Something I hadn't experienced for quite some time. It moved something deep inside of me, and for the first time in years, I crawled outside to reintroduce myself to the real world.

So here I sit today, somehow alive to tell you this story. And I don't tell you this to scare you, my friend. I don't tell you this to give you nightmares. I only tell you this to give you hope. Maybe I'm crazy, but deep down I believe that I wasn't the only one who suffered greatly from that disease called Pinterest. I wasn't the only one who sacrificed relationships and personal hygiene. Somewhere out there, an innocent soul is trapped amongst the cat pictures and inspirational quotes. And if my story can help that one person, then perhaps all of this was worth it.

My name is Alyssa J. Gibbs. I'm 18 years old. And I have survived the Pinterest Apocalypse.

~*~

About the Author:
Alyssa is from a little-bitty town in Illinois.
She loves Jesus, fashion, penguins, sprinkles, coffee, Australian accents, music, laughing, rainy days, and life in general. Her dream is to one day travel the world while reading good books, taking lots of pictures, and eating delicious food.

Glitter Girl

There's something enchanting about stepping into the mall and inhaling air sprinkled with that "new clothes" smell. Your favorite song is dancing on the radio airwaves, which puts you in the perfect mood to shop. You step into your favorite store, and a neon display of items is begging to find a home in your closet.

You're a glitter girl. You adore spending money on makeup, getting your nails done, and pretty much anything that sparkles, shimmers and shines. As girls, we love glitter gloss, perfume, high heels, hairspray and items that make us feel like we're sprinkled in pixie dust. But who can blame us? Who can resist stylish scarves, Chanel bags, bow rings, and the catchy song pumping out of Aeropostle?

There's something spectacularly satisfying about exiting your favorite store with pink bags of goodies. A girl can get a rush from finding the perfect pair of shoes. Just ask Cinderella!

The Urge to Splurge
I still remember my first trip to the mall. It was my eighth birthday. I proudly strutted down the narrow aisles that felt like a runway. My plaid purse hung over my shoulder. I held Mom's hand so I wouldn't get lost in the sea of shoppers. I was so ready for this. Loaded with birthday money, my anticipations were high. I had seen Mary-Kate and Ashley Olsen display the aura of amazingness which happens to every girl when she enters a mall. She instantly becomes cool.

I was never really interested in glitter and high heels, until I started watching every Olsen twin movie I could rent from the video store. Like stunning flashes of strobe lightning, I suddenly saw the image of two beautiful girls with flawless faces, dressed in the hottest jeans. The girls looked calm, cool and crazy confident. They were surrounded by friends, dancing with funky music and having the time of their lives. How could I not want that?

At age eight I discovered what being a girl was all about. I started to believe that teenage girl life revolved around makeup, clothes and boys; but mostly clothes.

I'm sure you've picked up on the same vibe. When did you first get the memo? Was it from your favorite collection of chick flicks, a Disney show you watched when you were young, or from the endless string of beauty advertisements on TV?

It's a tempting message. The models on magazine covers and the T.V. screen sure look like they're enjoying themselves. The life of the rich and famous is obviously delicious. To be pampered and primped with such glam and girliness all the time looks like a fairytale dream. Surely that's what being a girl is all about!

I quickly discovered that the high fashion, electrified glam world of my favorite starlets wasn't at all attainable. I chased it, but could never measure up. The more I shopped, the worse I felt. Can you relate? As girls, we have filled our shopping bags with all sorts of goodies, yet none of these things last or make us consistently happy. We buy T-shirts that get sweat stains, jeans get grass stains, and our shoes are ruined with mud from the rain.

It's a depressing thought, but all these items which we consume, eventually wither away. We're forever finding that what we bought yesterday is so...yesterday. The most devastating realization is that feeling that hits you when the shopping trip is over. You've tried on your clothes, modeled them for Instagram, and then...just like that...it's over.

Goodbye to the rush; the thrill of having new things. Now you have no money, and although you have a closet full of clothes, you still don't have enough. You've got nothing to wear! Why do we feel like this? Why that constant desire to have more? Why do we crave something that ten thousand pairs of shoes can never satisfy?

Glitz & Glam

Our favorite celebrities in Hollywood sure love glitter. We eagerly watch their Instagram feeds with updates on their nails. These starlets seem to be living an absolute dream life. These girls who have mall-sized closets have been blessed with many material items and amazing experiences. They date swoon-worthy movie stars and show off their favorite stilettos on the red carpet. Yet, for these girls who own like a billion pairs of shoes, they're still not satisfied.

So many of our favorite "stars" struggle with eating disorders and self-destructive activities. Though they appear to be living the dream, so many are caught up in a terrible nightmare.

When we hear stories like this, our jaws drop. How could a girl who has so much stuff feel like she has nothing? The girl could own every pair of wedge heels ever made! She could afford to wear all things cute and have any guy she liked! Yet somewhere, beneath it all, she was miserable.

It's all-too-easy to paste on a smile, play the part of perfection, and quietly crumble to pieces.

Sleeping Beauty, It's Time to Awaken

Do you remember the childhood fairy tale of Sleeping Beauty? After touching a forbidden spindle, she fell into a deep sleep. She was tucked into a stone tower so lofty, the walls couldn't be scaled by any man. Suffocating weeds subtly entangled Sleeping Beauty's wrists, wrapping themselves around her hands and feet like tight chains.

Sometimes we can feel like Sleeping Beauty. Locked up within something so much bigger than ourselves. In the heart of every girl, there is a desire to be deeply loved and set free from what holds us back. We all want our lives to be something more than what we have known and seen. Our childhood dreams beckon us to arise and live glorious lives, but suffocating pain keeps us from moving an inch. We have a desire to live a spectacular, splendorous, out of this world life...but we've all discovered that it can't be found in a shopping mall, on a TV show, or in a boyfriend's arms.

So many of us are masters at appearing as though we are living in a sweet dream world, when in reality, we're caught up in the middle of a nightmare.

But is there really such a person as Prince Phillip, who will come and save us? Is there really a man brave enough to rescue us from… ourselves?

The shocking truth is that no man or human prince can save a girl from herself. But what if there is something greater than man? What if there is a force more powerful that could bring about my rescue? To set me free from inner demons, I would need a powerful angel or god. A love that knows no limits, that is not bound by time or even galaxies. If my struggles and prisons are inside, I would require something unseen. Something bigger than myself. Something bigger than the dragon who desires to kill me.

Princess, what would you say if I told you I've found Him?

I've found One who makes brave Prince Phillip look wimpy in comparison to the true Hero of this story. I've found a Champion. A fearless warrior who overcame every known obstacle to man in order to rescue me. He is no son of Adam. He is a Heavenly Prince. Girls, to find the purpose for your existence and connect with your Creator, is the most amazing thing you'll ever experience.

We can try to fill ourselves up with so many things like shopping sprees, attention from guys, and affirmation from our friends. Yet in the midst of all this, we can still feel our hearts aching for something greater than what we have known. You know that you've been made for more. You hate feeling discouraged, depressed and empty. Don't you feel the longing in your heart? You want something. You need something. You need a Champion Dragon Slayer.

I'm sending out a memo to every captive Sleeping Beauty, a message sent by carrier pigeon that says,

"Don't believe the deceptive mirage. They're telling us what a girl's life should be; boys, clothes, and lip gloss...but it's not what it appears to be. The world's goodies leave you with a sugar high for ten seconds then slam you to an even lower place of devastation. We don't have to keep living like this! I've found the Prince, the Lord Jesus Christ. He is on His way. He defeated the very dragon who locked you in the tower. He's coming to awaken your heart with true love's first kiss. All you have to do is let Him in."

I don't know about you, but I plan on living a spectacular life! I want to make the most of the time I've been given. I don't want to chase lip gloss, skinny jeans, and Prada bags that can't make me happy, and won't fill up that "God space" inside. Girls, I want the real deal.

~*~

10 Trendy Shopping Tips

1) Yesterday Is In

The whimsical vintage looks of yesterday are once again appearing on the runways. Pick a decade, any decade! The 50s, 60s, and 70s influences are appearing in the mall. Choose your favorite time period and incorporate some of yesterday's classic pieces into tomorrow's next big trend!

2) Try A Funky Color Combo Like Pink & Brown

When I was a young girl, my Mom told me never to wear pink and red together. Who says we have to follow the color rules? Fashion today is screaming that wild colors are in. So go for what you like! Try a funky color combo like pink and brown, or gray and pink.

3) Know Where To Find What You Want

It's important to become familiar with who sells what, where you can find the best quality and how much money you'll be spending.

Discount stores like TJ Maxx & Marshall's sell brand names for discount prices. You can spend less money there than you would walking into a brand name store. But, it can also be harder to find what you want if searching for a specific piece. These sale stores make the shopping experience feel like a sophisticated garage sale. It's a classy step up from Goodwill, but if you like treasure hunts, you can find some real deals!

Brand name stores like Gap & Banana Republic are pricier, but may make it easier to find what you're looking for if you have a specific item in mind.

Target & Wal-Mart are discount department stores which offer low prices and only provide the clothes their companies and labels make.

Department stores like Macy's & Sears provide their own brand names at a pretty good price. The stores themselves are sometimes fancier, cleaner and all around nicer.

4) Purchase In The Off Season

Savvy shoppers know that going bargain hunting for the pieces they need in the off season will save them a chunk of change! For example, in the Fall, check out the clearance rack to begin putting together next year's summer wardrobe! Do the same in the summer, when those winter clothes are on sale. You'll be amazed by how much money you can save!

5) Be A Smart Accessorize-er

It's hard not to snatch up every adorable scarf, hat, necklace and ring we see...but a girl can spend so much money on accessories that pretty soon she finds she has too many to wear all at once! Is your jewelry box tangled with jewels you never wear anymore? Do you have scarves that match nothing in your wardrobe? It might be time to smarten up when you accessorize. Seek out items that will go with more than one outfit in your closet, (at least three!) and try to resist the urge to spend money on something just because it's cute. Be practical. Think twice, and you'll discover that you might not need as much as you think you do.

6) Make A List

To avoid spending money on what you really don't need, make a list before you hit the mall. Keep in mind your specific goals for that shopping trip. Are you Christmas shopping for a friend? Do you need new socks and a pair of tennis shoes? If you know you don't need a new purse, then stay from the accessories and things that might tempt you away from what your goal is! Also, know what your budget for that particular shopping trip is. Only bring what you want to spend! When your money is gone, there will be no more temptations to splurge!

7) Should I Take Two?

Every girl has that moment where she feels like she's found the PERFECT top, pair of jeans or skirt. Next time you have that moment, and you totally love it, take advantage of it. Why not buy two of the same thing, just in different colors? Who is going to notice anyway?

8) Have At Least One Cute Dress For Special Occasions
Next time you have some extra spending money for clothes, why not check out the dress rack? It's a great idea to have at least one cute dress for special occasions. I used to feel like handing over a hunk of change for a dress I would only wear once (like to a wedding or graduation party) would be a waste. But you'll be surprised at how often occasions arise where Cinderella needs something cute to wear!

9) Be A Classic, Not A Trend
Trends come and go, but some forever pieces will always be in. Make sure you have some of the classic items that never go out of style. Jeans, jean jackets, leggings, tank tops for layering, black pants, and dressy flats will always come in handy.

10) Out With The Old & In With The New!
Don't be a clothing hoarder. When your closet is stuffed full of so many clothes that you don't have enough days on the calendar to wear them, it's time to pass them on to someone who needs them more than you do. Your local clothing pantry at church, Salvation Army, or Goodwill are some great alternatives. A younger sibling or cousin might also enjoy the benefits of your yesterday clothes!

~*~

Her Adequacy

So many times in life we feel inadequate - our pasts hanging in the back of our mind and our flaws focusing in on us like a sharp shooter. Some days we feel beautiful and some days we do not. This roller coaster of emotions drives us crazy and we wonder, "Will I ever feel beautiful again?"

You *will* and you *are*.

Our worth has been under attack from the evil one since the Garden of Eden. The serpent lied to Eve, telling her that if she ate the forbidden fruit she would be like God. But WAIT. She was already like God. She was made in His image. The man and woman both were made in God's likeness. The enemy began to make her doubt her worth by planting lies in her mind. If he could make her doubt her worth, he could cause her to give up her position of royalty. Due to believing these lies, she gave up her position as a princess of God. Satan is the father of lies and he wants to take away our position as daughters of God. He will send people or things to discourage us. Hurtful words from others can really do damage to our identity if we do not know who we are and whose we are. It is important that we listen to Jesus and Jesus alone! There are many voices pulling on us every day: friends, family, media, our own mind, and the enemy. This is why the Apostle Paul wrote in Romans 12:2 saying,

"Be not conformed to this world: but be transformed by the renewing of your mind, that ye may prove what is that good, acceptable, and perfect will of God."

Everything you do flows from what you think. If we think like the world and not like Christ, we cannot know or live in God's will for our lives. That is why Paul told the Church of Rome to let God transform them by renewing the way they think. How do we do this? We must consume our minds and hearts with Jesus. As we begin to live our lives before Jesus, always seeking Him and loving Him, our hearts begin to long for what

He longs for, and our thoughts line up with His Word.

Abba Father wants you to know your worth. He does not want you seeking it from people or things. The only way to know your worth is to know the One who gives it! Are you daily getting to know Jesus better? Are you reading His Word and applying it to your life? Jesus is your Prince, and He desires that you truly live in peace. Apart from Him there is no peace, and there is no worth. He came to give life and life more abundantly. Depression and fear are NOT a part of God's plan for His children. Fear is a spirit, and the Word says,

For God has not given us a spirit of fear but of power, love, and a sound mind.

The original Greek meaning for the word "sound" is the word sozo. Sozo in Greek means wholeness, healing, deliverance, and salvation. This is the same word used in John 3:17, where Jesus said He came that the world might be saved. Jesus came not just to save you from sin, but to heal you from its effects upon your life. His death means you can now think and live in the light of His love! No more fear. No more insecurity. No more lies. You have a new identity!

You can now be confident no matter what you have done, because Jesus has made you pure through His blood on the cross. He has covered you with His radical, unending, beautiful love. His love has made you beautiful! So yield to Him all the contents of your heart. Offer up to Him your hurts, your past mistakes, your present struggles, and everything you do not understand. Ask Him to heal your heart from any wounds people have inflicted upon you. Forgive those that have attacked you and bless them with your mouth (Matthew 5). Jesus is your healing. He is your rest, and He makes all things new in His presence.

Give yourself to Him and as you do, He will mend your brokenness and give you beauty for ashes. No one can stay the same in the presence of Jesus, for He is life, healing, peace, joy, and love. I know how it feels to be broken, but I know that my brokenness does not faze Him. He is bigger than my pain!

Here are some simple ways to find renewed confidence and worth in Jesus:

Worship Him: Turn on your favorite worship music and pour out your heart before Him. Peace will flood your heart, and He will speak His love over you!

Read the Word of God: The Bible is God's written words! There are truths in the Word that will set you free, once you believe them and speak them over your life. Ask God to lead you by His Spirit to what He wants to say to you in His Word. He will speak when you ask and believe! This will help your mind to think His thoughts instead of the lies of the enemy.

Talk with Jesus: Prayer is simply talking with God. When you talk things out with Him and cry out before Him, He will bring His healing to your heart. Prayer is power when we believe in the one we are talking to! Jesus wants your pain; tell Him about it. Jesus wants to embrace you!

Renounce the lies: When the enemy or people speak negative things into your life, refuse to listen to them and counterattack the lie with truth. When the enemy says to you that you are not beautiful, say, "I am fearfully and wonderfully made! I may not feel beautiful but I am! Jesus makes no mistakes." Your heart and mind will line up with your words.

Meditate on beautiful things: Do not relive your past in your mind. This is easier said than done, but when you meditate on the wrong things you feel the wrong things. What you feel is a product of what you think. Think about it... if you think about your struggles and your past mistakes it will discourage you, but if you think about His love for you it will empower you. You cannot rise above what you think and believe. God is doing so much healing and restoration in my heart through these simple tools. Song of Solomon, Psalms, Isaiah, John, Ephesians, Colossians, Galatians, and Philippians are just a few encouraging books of the Bible that will lift you up as you read them!

You are loved, pursued, wanted, cherished, and forgiven. Jesus is your adequacy. You are enough in Him for He has paid the highest price! Rest in His love that your joy may be full (John 15). Here is a sample prayer, to help release your heart from fear, into faith to believe what God says about you:

"Abba Father, I thank you for Your Son Jesus and the price He paid. His death paid for my complete freedom! I give my heart, mind, and body to Jesus. I yield to His complete control over my life! I choose to think His thoughts and meditate on His love for me. I am not what the world says that I am or what even people say I am. I am loved. I am cherished. I am wanted. I am righteous in Christ Jesus. I have the mind of Christ, and I listen to His Word alone! I forgive those that have hurt me and release them to you! Thank you for healing my heart and removing any bitter root. Give me a passion for your presence and a passion for your Word. Make me into the woman I am called to be. I am Yours! I choose you now and for eternity in Jesus name! Amen! Be blessed, Princess of God!

About the Author:
Nellie Martin was born and raised in North Georgia. She fell in love with Jesus when she was fourteen, and her life has never been the same. She is attending college at Bethel School of Supernatural Ministry. She loves children, drinking coffee, and shopping! Check out Nellie's amazing blog: hisladiesinwaiting.wordpress.com

The Secret is Out!
Interview with Kylie Bisutti!

Get to know the former Victoria's Secret model who traded seductive photo shoots for a runway with a greater purpose and calling: a role model shining brightly for Christ!

Crown of Beauty: As a young girl growing up you were teased at school for being "too skinny" and "too tall." These traits were perfect for the modeling industry, and it sounds as if you fit right in when you started pursuing jobs in the industry as a teen. Why did you choose to start modeling?

Kylie: Originally I wanted to become a model because I thought that the models had it made. They seemed to be so confident, and they were considered beautiful by the world. They got lots of attention, and it seemed very glamorous. I was so hurt by people bullying me, and I wanted to prove to them that I was worthy.

COB: Once involved with fully pursuing your modeling career, you were told by your agency that you needed to shed some weight in order to book modeling jobs. I have to admit that this part of your story shocked me! I mean you were so stunning, thin, and a perfectly healthy weight...and someone wanted you a size smaller! How did this affect your self-esteem?

Kylie: It affected me in a really bad way. My mind became warped, and when I would look in the mirror I would just cry and think I needed to lose weight. I wasn't really seeing myself and how thin I truly was. I ended up getting down to 108 lbs. and still thought I wasn't thin enough. I developed a lot of body image issues.

COB: Why do you think you continued modeling even though it was negatively affecting the way you thought about yourself?

Kylie: I continued for a lot of reasons...My own pride of being afraid of what others would think if I didn't continue modeling in New York and came home a failure... along with my desire to have attention and be famous. I was basically living for my idols rather than living for Christ. I also thought that if I made it big one day that things would be different, and I wouldn't be critiqued so much about my body.

COB: At age nineteen you beat out 10,000 other women who all had the same dream, and won a Victoria's Secret modeling contest! You earned your "angel wings" and were offered money, fame, and attention on a silver platter. How did you feel at that point? How did your life change after winning this competition?

Kylie: At that point it was a dream come true and the pinnacle of my career. It was also one of the most insecure times of my life. My life changed completely after winning. My status in the industry was at a whole new level, and I was instantly thrown into a world of craziness.

COB: Over a period of time, God started dealing with your heart and caused you to question what you were doing with your life. He showed you that your lifestyle and career was having a negative effect on young girls. I understand that a young girl in your life, your cousin actually, told you she wanted to quit eating so that she could be "pretty like you." How did her words affect you? Is that what caused your heart to begin to change?

Kylie: God has used her words in a huge way in my life. He showed me that what I was doing in my career was causing her and many other little girls to feel insecure and not worthy. He showed me that the type of role model I was being was causing girls a lot of pressure and was promoting the standard of beauty that the media has set. He opened my eyes to all of these things and began to work in my heart over time! Now I want girls to know that everything they see in magazines is just an illusion and an impossible standard of beauty for anyone, and that they don't have to feel the pressures that the media puts on them. This is one of my biggest reasons for writing *I'm No Angel*.

COB: Something that strikes me about your story and so encourages me is that once God started showing you that He was calling you to a higher standard of life purity and to be an example for the girls in your life, you obeyed. You chose to stop modeling in lingerie and participating in provocative photo shoots. You walked away from a multi-million-dollar opportunity only to be criticized and called crazy by so many people! But you obeyed God's voice anyway! How difficult was it to actually follow through with what God was showing you?

Kylie: It was surprisingly easier than I thought it would be. I had such an amazing peace about the decision. One that I had never felt before about my career. It was the kind of peace I had in my heart when I married Mike. Like I knew 100% that it was God's plan for me and that it was right.

COB: One of our favorite verses is Titus 2:2-5 which says, "Likewise, teach the older women to be reverent in the way they live, not to be slanderers or addicted to much wine, but to teach what is good. Then they can urge the younger women to love their husbands and children, to be self-controlled and pure, to be busy at home, to be kind, and to be subject to their husbands, so that no one will malign the word of God." This verse describes the big sister role, and how we as Christians are called to live before our little sisters in Christ - as a role model. How fulfilling is it to be able to speak into young girls' lives and share your story? Do you get joy and fulfillment from doing that?

Kylie: It is so fulfilling. More fulfilling than all of the modeling jobs or money and fame that the modeling world gave me. I get so much joy out of sharing my heart with girls, and seeing how God uses my experiences and what I have gone through to impact them! I'm so thankful that this is the path He has for my life and that He is using me in this way!

COB: What advice do you have for girls who might not be in the modeling industry or be on a big stage before fans and followers, but still want to be a good role model for their little sisters in Christ?

Kylie: God can use you in so many wonderful ways to be a good role model! It doesn't matter if you have a bunch of followers or a big platform. I encourage you to pray to God that He opens up doors for you where you can be a light and a good example, and that He brings girls into your life who you can encourage and show love to!

COB: Why do you think it's important for young women to have a standard of modesty? Obviously we're not going to go to school wearing lingerie or pose in our underwear for photo shoots....but what about short shorts, and low-cut tops? Do those "not-so-harmful" pieces of clothing have an effect on the guys in our lives?

Kylie: They will definitely have an effect on the guys in your lives...And it will be a negative one. By dressing immodestly we are displaying our bodies as a temptation for our brothers in Christ, and we are also not showing people Christ in the way that we dress. The Bible says to honor God in the way we dress, and we really should examine our hearts to see why we are wearing the things we do. Is it to get attention from guys? Or to honor God? This is why I think it is important to have a standard of modesty!

COB: What advice would you offer your young cousin or any other girl who came up to you with tears streaming down her face saying, "I hate myself. I want to be pretty. I don't like who I am."? How can a girl truly believe that she is beautiful and be comfortable with who she is?

Kylie: My message to girls is that God made you the way you are, and He looks at the beauty of the heart! He thinks you are beautifully made. It's better to focus on that than on what others think of you here on earth, because we will spend eternity with him versus a short period of time with the people who reject us here on earth. Here we are told that we need to change in order to be beautiful, but in Christ we find that he accepts and loves us with all of our flaws and everything the world would call ugly. When you start seeing yourself the way God sees you and not the way society tells you are, you will truly feel beautiful.

~*~

Did You Know...
The prayers of Kylie's husband were used to change her heart. While she was modeling for Victoria's Secret, Mike petitioned the Lord in prayer, on behalf of his girl.

"The prayer of a righteous man is powerful and effective."
{James 5:16}
Just think...your future husband might be praying for you too!

~*~

Visit www.kyliebisutti.com and learn more about her story, grab a copy of her book, *I'm No Angel*, and check out her "God Inspired Fashion" line!

Becoming Esther: For Such a Time as This

Before Esther became a Queen, she was just a young woman like us. She was an orphan girl with a heart full of high hopes and dreams. She probably had the same desires and fears that we have. I'm sure she went through days of doubt, not knowing what her purpose was going to be in life. Little did she know that she was chosen and predestined. She was about to walk into the incredible destiny that God had prepared for her, but it took a little time. She still had to learn, grow and prepare herself as a woman before she could ever enter into that next phase of being a wife and Queen.

When Esther and the virgins were summoned into the palace to possibly be chosen as the next queen, the Bible says that she had to complete 12 months of beauty treatments; six months in oil of myrrh and six months with perfumes and cosmetics. Esther had to learn the ways of the Kingdom before she could ever unite with what God had for her. Those 12 months were life changing for her and who knows what God revealed to her in that time, but she found her purpose. Her heart was transformed. She became a woman of faith and of excellence, but the process was difficult.

I can't imagine how discouraging it was to her heart at times, seeing her promise before her every day but not being able to receive it. Yet she never lost hope. Esther believed in what most people thought was impossible!

God's timing was perfect for her life, and in all those 12 months of waiting and preparing, God was not only working on Esther's heart, He was working on the King's heart. When that night finally came to go unto the King, the anointing was all upon her and He saw that. She obtained grace and favor in his sight and completely captivated his heart. He put the royal crown upon HER head and made her queen. That was the moment she had prepared so long for, and it was worth the wait. Every day of Esther's life, God was shaping her for that very special moment. She became Esther, before she was Esther!

She went on to be one of the most courageous and anointed women in the Bible. Her story of preparation and saving the Jewish people has become an incredible example to many generations, especially to many single women like myself. From the very beginning, God had a plan for her, and because of her faithfulness, He blessed her not only with the man of her dreams but with such an amazing, blessed life.

Like Esther, many of us have that same longing to find that man who will sweep us off our feet and that we'll have that happily ever after with. When we were being formed in our mothers' womb, God breathed that desire in our spirits to want to be wives and mothers someday. That's all we ever dream of, but we lack patience, and sometimes we can get so caught up in that dream that we take our eyes off God and choose less than His best. We tend to waste this time of singleness, when we should be cherishing every second of it! God is wanting us to use this time to prepare like Esther, to learn HIS ways before we are joined to the heart that we are destined to be with.

That's why this time of singleness is precious! It's a time to cultivate beauty and build virtue. A time to let God transform our hearts NOW, so that we can be the virtuous woman that our one day husband needs. But how do we become like that? By being crazy faithful to Jesus, in that secret place communing with Him and letting Him teach us how to be that Proverbs 31 and Titus 2 woman. Ladies: When we're in the presence of God there is not only an INWARD change, but an OUTWARD change, because it will show such a RADIANT BEAUTY.

There is nothing more beautiful than a woman who is God-fearing, virtuous, gentle, kind, and passionately in love with Jesus. The right man will cherish and protect that! Just like the Lord, that man will see your heart and not just your outward appearance. I'm not saying that your outward appearance isn't important though, because it is. I do believe as women of God it is very important that we take care of the temple we've been blessed with. There's nothing wrong with putting on a little makeup and dressing up. Even Esther prepared with perfumes and cosmetics. So that's a part of being a lady, but don't think that your worth is valued by any of that. You are fearfully and wonderfully made! Your price is far above rubies, and you shouldn't be treated any less.

Don't be discouraged if you're still single! God has a reason for it, and it's just not time yet for you to meet your Prince. God may be keeping you in the palace for a little bit longer, because there might be a few things you still need to learn. Remember, God makes ALL THINGS beautiful in HIS TIME. If you remain faithful to Him, He will remain faithful to you! Every season in life has beauty and wonder of its own, so be content. Stay focused, and before you know it your promise will be before your feet.

~*~

About the Author:
Kenya-Nicole Gossett has been in full-time ministry her whole life. The Lord graced her to go on her first missions trip at the age of 16 months, and since then she has traveled and lived abroad 22 times, doing the work of ministry.

The Lord gave her the vision for "Becoming Esther," a ministry that would raise up young women in the fear of the Lord, keeping them pure until marriage and teaching them to prepare themselves, not only for their Heavenly King but for their husbands as well. The ministry has gone into several nations including Kenya, Philippines, India, Pakistan and Myanmar.

Follow them on Twitter & Instagram: @BecomingEsther
And visit their website, becomingesther.org

2+2=4

I stared at the scale and shuddered. Half of me wanted (a desperate, clutching want) to step on and see what it had to say. Half of me didn't want to see it.

In my mind, it was simple. Just as 2+2=4, so the number on the scale + the number of guys that checked me out = my worth. My worth as a human being.

I was always insecure. It wasn't overwhelming in high school, but even then I never felt like I measured up.

By the time I got to college, I was starting to feel more confident. And then I started dating this guy. A guy who thought I wasn't pretty enough. Wasn't skinny enough. Wasn't godly enough. Wasn't quiet enough. Wasn't stylish enough. One day he even said, "Sometimes I feel like you're worthless."

We dated for two years, because I was head over heels and didn't have the courage to break it off and face the world alone. Without a guy on my arm, who was I? When the relationship ended, I dove headlong into the one thing I'd been eying for so long: Beauty.

The Wrong Equation
I was insecure about EVERYTHING...grades, church involvement, popularity, clothes, hair, face...you name it, I wasn't good enough. But it all boiled down to one small thing I tried to control, or rather, one thing that was never small enough - my weight.

My relationship with the scale was an abusive one. It made me laugh and told me I was good enough when I was thin enough. It made me want to cry and do awful things to myself when I gained half a pound. It told me who I was and what I was worth. And I listened.
But here's the thing:
Numbers on a scale can't tell you how funny you are.

Numbers on a scale can't tell you the meaningful relationships you have in your life.

Numbers on a scale can't tell you that your eyes light up when you smile.

Numbers on a scale can't tell you how much God loves you.

There was a song I loved by *Barlow Girl* that said,
"Mirror, mirror, on the wall, have I got it?
Cause mirror you've always told me who I am
I'm finding it's not easy to be perfect
So sorry, you don't define me..."

My mirror couldn't define me, just like numbers on a scale couldn't define me. They weren't a 2+2=4 equation for my worth. Their equation read something like 1+1=5. Um, *wrong.*

A Love I Can't Earn
One night I came home to try and "make something happen" in my time with God. I was going to "pray up a storm" and "read my Bible apart" and invent a magical moment that would prove to God I was a daughter He could be proud of, just as I was always trying to prove to myself I was good enough.

But that night I felt in my heart that God wanted me to lie down, not say a word, and listen to the song "Oh How He Loves."

So I listened. For forty-five minutes I listened. "Oh how He loves us." "Oh, oh how He loves us." "How He loves us, oh." Again and again.

I heard my Heavenly Father whisper, "I just want you to be with Me."

In the coming weeks, months, and years, this was the message He repeatedly spoke to me: "Tiffany, you're trying so hard to impress Me. But I'm not impressed by how good you are; your best deeds are like filthy rags. You can never earn My love, but I've given it to you freely. I don't delight in how spiritual you are; I delight in you. I don't delight in how pretty you are; I delight in you. I don't delight in how good you are;

I delight in you. I don't love you because you're good enough; I love you because you're my daughter. And nothing can ever change that."

It's hard for me to grasp. I can't control this love; I can only receive it.

The Source of Worth
I felt like I was earning praise from the numbers on the scale. I felt like I could control it. Eventually it spiraled out of control and left me empty and broken. But I couldn't earn my Father's unconditional love. I couldn't work harder to make it greater. He delighted in me simply because I was His daughter.

Our worth is not determined by the numbers on a scale, or the number of guys that check us out, or the percentage of our grade, or the sum total of our popularity, or even the amount of our spirituality. Our worth only comes from the Father who created us; the Father we will spend eternity with.

I know the scale cannot give me my worth, so I don't listen to it anymore. I haven't listened to it in so long, that it no longer makes me tremble, and I can't hear its demanding voice. It doesn't make me laugh or cry.

But when I'm alone with God, that's when I laugh with delight at the depth of His love for me. That's when I cry realizing that even when I feel unworthy, His love doesn't change, and His love makes me worthy.

He loves the way my eyes light up when I smile. That's why He made them that way. He reminds me of how many loving relationships He's put in my life. I'm pretty sure He gets a kick out of my humor and personality. And He always reminds me - *always* - how much He loves me.

Yesterday I was laying on my bed pouring out my heart to God, and I felt like He was smiling on me. My heart could have burst with knowing how much He delighted in simply having me close to Him. I felt like I was wrapped in a bear hug.

When we know the love of Christ, it changes everything. Because just as 2+2=4, so His love defines our true worth and identity.

~*~

About the Author:
To hear the rest of Tiffany Dawn's story and how she found freedom from her quest for beauty, check out The *Insaitable Quest for Beauty* book and discover her amazing ministry!
www.tiffanydawn.net

Redefining the Face of Beauty
Meet Emily: Founder of Verity Varee

Crown of Beauty: What inspired you to begin Verity Vareé?

Emily: Oh my goodness, so many things. I've always loved fashion. From the time I was a little girl, I paid close attention to the fashion industry and its influence on our culture. As I grew older, I fell in love with the various aspects of the fashion industry, i.e. makeup artistry, modeling, styling, location scouting, wardrobe, and magazines chock-full of beautiful images. I used to make collages all the time, kept journals, wrote about trends I noticed, and still have a childlike obsession with glitter. When I was 16, I began modeling professionally and was thrown into all the glamour, stress, and endless excitement that the fashion world had to offer. I loved it. Learning the art of modeling, continuing on to become a makeup artist, then dreaming of styling my own sets gave me ideas of starting a magazine/blog of my adventures.

It was sometime in the middle of my modeling/acting career that I began to feel an emptiness. I couldn't explain it. It was as if all I'd ever dreamed of felt hollow and tiresome. My dreams became demands in my own head. No longer was I doing what I loved, I was doing what I had to do to survive in a world where someone else determined my beauty. I'd known from the beginning that the fashion industry was not always an uplifting place, and I went into it with that mindset seeking to be an example of truth and health to others, but it was easier said than done. I started to feel like a bag of bones with no purpose or support. I took a short break from professional modeling and started to ask myself some honest, hard questions like, "What is beauty? Do I believe I am beautiful? Does my story matter? Do other women feel this way?" The answers to those questions are what inspired me to create Verity Vareé.

COB: Tell us about a "Reveals" photo shoot and what that entails.

Emily: A Reveal is the process each woman goes through in telling her story, both visually through photos and auditory through a recorded interview with me, the writer. Her first photo shoot is all natural, no makeup, no special hairstyling, in her everyday clothing to show her in the most natural state possible. The idea is that she is beautiful as she is. Beauty is inherent in every woman, not something to be attained, or worked for. Further still, her interview tells us all about that woman (her loves, her dreams, her life story) and allows us to see beauty in the way she lives. The last part of the Reveal is a styled shoot where the woman chooses a theme (peacock queen, vintage garden party, fairy, and urban chic to name a few) and we work with her to create her dream photo shoot.

The longer we run, the more in depth we've been able to get with our ideas and styling. It's so exciting! This is the truly magical part of the shoot, because we give women the opportunity to express their personalities and natural beauty by using fashion and creativity as a tool for them, not *against* them, as it so often feels. All in all, the Reveal is comprised of natural photos, styled photos, and the woman's interview, telling each individual story with detail and care. It's a lot of work and a lot of fun. We do it all in one day, so it's an all-day-on-set affair!

COB: Why do you think people are so drawn to this project?

Emily: I think for most women there is still a little girl in them who wants to play dress up, be pampered, and create/star in her ultimate dream. However, not all of the women are girly, so I think the ultimate reason is that every woman wants to know what she is worth, or if she is worth anything at all. We want to know what we have to offer as people and as members of a fearfully competitive society. Telling your story, seeing photos of yourself, and having someone else allow you to see yourself through their eyes helps give you fresh perspective on who you are. It's like asking a friend, "What do you see in me?" and getting a full-fledged, detailed answer. There are also many women who feel called to share their stories as encouragement to others, who simply don't have a platform to do so, and they find the opportunity through Verity Vareé.

COB: The media has a distorted view of what "true beauty" is. What are you doing to change that perspective?

Emily: The Reveals on our website are used not only to showcase the woman in that particular story, but also to encourage other women and to challenge their perspective on beauty. One glance at a room full of women will show you that no two of us looks the same, but reading our

Reveal stories also shows you that no two of us should. I often use the illustration of a flower garden to describe how the media views beauty. When you walk into a garden you are dazzled by all the different flowers. The various shapes, sizes, colors, and needs make each one of them distinct and wonderful in their own unique way. Our culture holds up one flower, a daisy for example, and tells all the other flowers to look like that. If you're a rose who starts trying to look like a daisy, not only are you on an incessant mission to change your natural form, you are also missing out on the gift of beauty that is yours that is inherent.

Through featuring women as they are, as they choose to express themselves and as their life story illustrates, we are saying loud and clear that the most beautiful you is the you that embraces you and determines not to change, but focuses your efforts on being the best lily, daffodil, or bluebell you can be. The flower illustration is one my mom gave me when I was a little girl. I never knew how heavily it would impact me and so many other women!

COB: Share one of your favorite memories about either a photo-shoot, or feedback you got from a girl who was empowered by this project. How is this encouraging and strengthening girls in their walk with God, and simply in their own self-confidence?

Emily: That is the first full response I got from Verity Vareé, and it literally sent me soaring:

"After seeing (daughter's name) come home BEAMING, I realized that what you are doing is something I wish every single teen could experience. You are literally calling forth beauty, calling forth what was created by God for good...the same things that are so often stolen or distorted or wrecked by the enemy and the world. Beauty is GOOD, and as I was looking at your website tonight and seeing her story, I just felt my heart leap. Seriously, you captured her spirit. (Daughter's name) was glowing from the time I picked her up...she felt so understood. Thanks for lighting up her spirit again with bits of truth and real beauty." -Mom

Realizing that I was helping people feel the way I had always longed to feel was just about the best thing I could have asked for. Another incredible response was from an older woman who did a Reveal with us. She said telling her story and getting to share gave her hope, encouragement, and filled her with life. Any emails that are encouraging and true just send me to the stars. I can't properly express how fulfilling it is to know that I am a part of something so much bigger than myself. I'm not the creator of this truth about beauty, simply the messenger to a small audience through this creative pursuit. The encouragement and strengthening of women is simply this: When a woman does a Reveal with us she is literally claiming and shouting the truth, "I am beautiful."

~*~

Our lovely book cover photo was taken by LaRue Photography {www.facebook.com/jessicalaruephotogprahy}

We can't thank Verity Varee enough for letting us use their photo as our cover! Check out the beautiful *Reveals* and find out how you can book your own photo session, or simply learn more about this amazing project!

Give 'em the thumbs up at www.facebook.com/verityvaree and visit www.verityvaree.com for more info!

PART 2: BALL GOWNS {Living As Royalty}

Me? A Princess? Shut Up!

My all-time favorite movie has to be *The Princess Diaries*.

I'm sure you're familiar with the tale. Mia Thermopolis is a fifteen-year-old, socially-awkward teenager who can't see much past her bushy eyebrows. Her life consists of scootering up the hilly San Francisco terrain with her best friend Lily and crushing on the hunky high school jock who doesn't know she exists. Her drab existence in the suffocating halls of high school are all she's ever known.

Her greatest aim in life? "My goal in life is to be invisible. And I'm really good at it."

One day her long lost, British, tea-drinking Grandmother arrives and reveals the deeply-hidden family secret. Mia's late father was crown prince of a small European country. That means Mia is a Princess and will inherit the throne. Her reaction is like a classic Hallmark moment.

"Me…a…a princess? Shut up!"

Can you imagine the horror? Mia frequently threw up in Speech class, got sat on by other classmates, and tripped on thin air. Not much princess potential there! The writers for this movie script must have had a fun time painting the contrast between Mia's life and the idea of what princess life should look like.

One of my favorite scenes is when Mia examines herself in the mirror and sighs, "Well, as usual, this is as good as it's going to get."

By the time the final credits of this movie roll, I have laughed, cried and cheered Mia on. Every time, I watch in amazement as she is transformed into a woman who learned to use her voice, walk with confidence (well, most of the time) and fearlessly (or not so fearlessly) step into the role she had been called to.

This movie always inspires me. Mia is the type of princess I want to run up to and give a big old hug, shouting, "Thank you for being real!" There's nothing movie star glamorous or polished and fake about this princess. She didn't grow up in a whimsical castle, or have a long line of men waiting to court her in the parlor. I relate with the girl who trips and slams bottom first onto the bleachers, much more than I care to admit!

I suppose the reason why Mia is such a treasured character to me, is because royalty is my reality. Yeah, you heard me right. I'm an undercover Princess. I might wear a pair of casual blue jeans, sneakers, and a messy pony-tail, but beneath it all...I am a daughter of the King. My life is skillfully being woven together into the most exciting saga, as the Grand Author and Storyteller is magically pulling it all together.

Just like Princess Mia, I discovered my royal fate through a shocking announcement. It was as if a royal footman dressed in the vintage garb, complete with a white wig, showed up on my doorstep and handed me a sealed invite to a royal ball. My eyes feasted on the glorious invitation, which sparkled with gold glitter. The royal emblem declared it was from the courts of Heaven. I trembled as I read. The words resonated in my spirit, as if they were living, penetrating and changing something inside my heart. The exploration of this grand fairytale all started with these words;

"The true light that gives light to everyone was coming into the world. He was in the world, and though the world was made through him, the world did not recognize him. He came to that which was his own, but his own did not receive him. Yet to all who did receive him, to those who believed in his name, he gave the right to become children of God — children born not of natural descent, nor of human decision or a husband's will, but born of God." {John 1:9-13}

This open invitation was the start of a magnificent journey. I believed in the One who breathed life into me, therefore I was given the right to become royalty. I was a spiritual orphan rescued from a terrible fate. The punishment of Hell and torment because I had broken so many of the Kingdom's rules was hanging over my head like a storm cloud. My dark surroundings and hidden sins clung to me like a heavy fog until the day a glorious light broke in. The shining Prince, the Light of the World, Jesus Christ, rode into my life and transported me into a fairytale. But just like Mia's story, my life didn't radically change overnight. Me being royalty didn't instantly give me a car, a job, or a boyfriend. It didn't make me stunning and successful in the eyes of this world. In fact, it would be easy for an untrained eye to pass me by and not see a princess standing there. My surroundings and life situation were still the same. I still had struggles, hurts, fears and tribulations.

But something did change. I had an identity switch. The nature of my heart and the very blood coursing through my veins was washed with the divine blood of Christ. My entire DNA had changed! When I said, "Yes" to this royal invitation, the heavens started to buzz with activity. I became a citizen of Heaven.

I now have an address in a city where the streets are paved with gold. No city on earth could match its unfathomable wealth because it is the dwelling place of my royal Father. As a legal citizen from this upper class society, I have a rank and social status that none can match… Daughter of the King. I have a glorious bedroom waiting for me in the King's castle. Mia had to wait several years before she saw her regal bedroom suite. The same is true for me. I've never seen the room before…in fact; I've never been to my homeland.

I can only imagine what my Heavenly bedroom looks like. Is it nestled high in a tower? Does it have an indoor waterfall and stream that flows through from the Crystal Sea?

As a temporary visitor on this earth, I'm currently lodging in a humble home tucked off the highway. My surroundings are anything but glamorous. Sometimes, on my bad days, when the sky is overcast and circumstances are dreary, I grow very anxious about my future. I know that I am guaranteed a happily ever after, and an eternal place in my Father's house…but what happens until then?

It's tempting at times, to shed my royalty identity and settle into the rhythm of an average American teenage girl. This earthly culture flashes glamorous images of fame, wealth and beauty. Sometimes I desire to chase their definition of worldly success. My royal identity is something unseen and it doesn't gain me much applause or affirmation from the world. Sometimes, I wish I could simply slip on a wig like Hannah Montana and conform to my jaded surroundings, just like a chameleon. It certainly would be easier.

But like Mia, I have discovered that attempting to mix the words average and extravagant into the same sentence, let alone the same life, can be extremely challenging. Continuing to think like an average girl, when I have been called to an extravagantly royal existence just doesn't work. Lilly urged Mia to take full advantage of the opportunity being handed to her: "You know, you being a princess is kind of a miracle."

Mia didn't quite see things that way. She asked Lilly to explain what was so great about her life being flipped upside down. Lilly explained the disappointing truth that her cable show only reached five people. She had little to no influence. But Mia? She had real power. A priceless opportunity. "Having the power to affect change and make people listen? What more of a miracle do you want?""

Grandmother Clarisse didn't force Mia into the job. But if she refused to take the crown, someone else would. There was a usurper lurking in the shadows, hoping to pounce on the power. (Mr. and Mrs. Barron. Remember the postage-stamp nose lady?) The same is true of us, if we abandon our royal crown, there is an enemy waiting to take possession of it.

Just like Mia, we have a choice to make. Will we take a step of faith toward our royal calling and receive the invitation into the King's courts? Or will we shrink back in fear with inadequate feelings of hopelessness, settling for our drab Americanized lives?

Boldly choosing to respond to our call as Daughters of the King will powerfully influence the lives of those around us. When we seek the Kingdom of Heaven and the One who rules, ask to learn His secrets, and live according to His royal law on the earth, we get to partner with Christ and live out the most amazing, exhilarating, epic story ever told! Sisters, I pray that these words stir something in your soul. If it is hope, or excitement, let it rise. If it is a vast discomfort and disgust with the way things have always been...let it surface. You are a princess. You have a destiny, a hope, and a future. It's okay to let feelings of discontentment arise! You're in the middle of a major mental shift. Mia had to work through this as well...

If you feel like you've been cheated, lied to, and have walked in anything less than the fullness of who you were created to be...that's because you were. The enemy knows you were created for royal greatness, and he has tried to keep you from understanding that. But now is the time to rejoice!

Get excited and determined! You are no longer ignorant to this call of brilliant greatness on your life! If you partner with Christ to pursue His heart and His Kingdom...you will be unstoppable!

Let us walk together and encounter our Royal King. Doing so will forever change the way we see Him, ourselves and the world around us. Let's refuse to let fear keep us from embracing our calling. In the past we have forfeited our royal authority to the enemy by:

A) Choosing to seek the world and all its flashy, neon-light pleasures for fulfillment, rather than God.

B) Being ignorant of what we've been given in Christ, and of our royal identity.

C) Falling in love with this culture, subscribing to their ideals, and conforming to the world around us.

Mia asked Joe, her security guard, "Can't I simply quit?"
Joe replied, "You can quit the job...but you can never stop being who you truly are...a princess."

It's a daily struggle, to live aware of the unseen and pursue the Kingdom of Christ. We get distracted by so many sparkly and shiny things that demand our attention. We daily abandon God's word for pleasure and enjoyment and quite often choose the easiest path rather than the high road. With each passing day, life reveals the loyalty of my heart or lack thereof. As a Princess carrying the name of Christ and the desires of my Father, am I willing to suffer temporary stings like persecution, discomfort, and people rolling their eyes behind my back? Am I willing to stand up against the voices that say, "Why don't you just do things our way?" Or do I care more about what man thinks of me, than pleasing the King?

Refusing to live out the call as His Royal Ones and powerfully influence this earth, makes us terrible stewards of what we've been given. I often forget who I am and who God is in my life. When distractions enrapture my heart, I forget about the unseen Kingdom that I have been called to.

One way that I manage do to this quite brilliantly is through worrying.

Majoring on the scene and obsessing over uncontrollable details such as what my future holds, finances, who I'll be marrying, the next book I'll write, if people like me or not, and if my ministry will be effective, etc. Quite often I take a microscope and examine my life. I start biting my nails. Too bad that just like Mia, sometimes I can't see past my big bushy eyebrows of worry.

I need to spend more time looking at the unseen, so that I do not forget who God is, what He has planned, and who I am in Christ! Often I need to remind myself of His unbridled goodness, and direct my eyes upward. Just look at all the Father has given us! We have a 24/7, all-access backstage pass into the very throne room of God! We can enter any time we need, crawl up on his lap, and ask Him anything. We have His undivided attention.

Jesus told us, "But seek first his kingdom and his righteousness, and all these things will be given to you as well." Matthew 6:33

How often do we spend time seeking His kingdom? What does that even look like? To seek the Kingdom is to seek the King. Jesus is the heartbeat of the Kingdom. He has so much to reveal about who He is, who we are in Him, and what He desires to do on the earth. As His royal ones, we must take time out of our busy schedules to incline our ears and ask what He desires to speak to our hearts.

"I have much more to say to you, more than you can now bear. But when he, the Spirit of truth, comes, he will guide you into all the truth. He will not speak on his own; he will speak only what he hears, and he will tell you what is yet to come." {John 16:12-13}

I cannot think of a better place to begin pursuing the King and responding to His invitation, than to dive into His Word! Jesus is the Word {John 1:14}, His Word is alive and active {Hebrews 4:12}, and He wants to speak to us today!

Dear Lord,
Thank You for sending your Son Jesus, so that I could be forgiven of sin
and adopted into your royal family. Thank You for specifically creating
me to be a Princess and to partner with Christ as a Royal Citizen of
Heaven! It blows my mind. Reveal more to my heart about this truth. Use
this time of prayer and reading your Word to speak to me. Show me what
it means to be your royal daughter. Strengthen me to pursue You and
Your Kingdom. Teach me Holy Spirit!
In Jesus Name.

Faith In Action...
Worrying is one of the worst things a princess can do. It displays distrust
in the Father and tells Him where our faith really lies...in ourselves and
what we can control.
Read these verses about worrying and ask the Lord to help you trust
Him.
Matthew 6: 25-34, Psalm 37:1-8, Philippians 4:4-7.

~*~

Royal Training

I cannot think of a greater honor than entering the throne room of the King of Kings. Yet, to be honest, I don't spend nearly as much time there as I should. Quite often, I'm a princess who runs off, worries her way out of His castle, knocks her tiara off in frantic fear, and rips her dress on a sharp branch called the cares of this world. I can search for so many things, and so many people to fill me up and steady my heart. Yet, unless I find my identity and joy in the throne room of the King, I am utterly disappointed.

As Princesses, many of us don't know how to linger or abide in His presence. We send up a five minute prayer, read a Psalm or two, stick our Bible on the shelf then hop on Pinterest. Day after day, we forfeit our time with the King, for time with a world who doesn't really care about us. Why do we do this?

Quite often, it's because we don't know what to do, or how to act in the stillness of our bedrooms, alone with an invisible God.

Here's a list of creative ideas to encourage your heart to seek after the One True King. Don't just read this list and think, "Awe, that sounds fun." Set down this book and run to the secret place of the Most High. Put these ideas into action. Stretch your quiet time from five minutes, to fifteen, to an hour, to three hours. Passionately pursue the One who gave everything for you. You will never once regret a moment spent alone with Him.

Creative Ways to Pursue the King
~Start a prayer journal. Write letters to God. Talk about your day. Spill out your heart in writing.

~Sing a worship song to the Lord, with your favorite CD. (Who says you need to be at church?!)

~Open up the book of Psalms and sing a worship song to Him. Your voice is your instrument. He loves to hear you break into song! Make it up as you go along!

~Choose 5 people you love, and pray scripture verses over them. Praying the Word is so much better than trying to think of things on our own. Jesus loves when we repeat His own words to Him!

~Brew a cup of coffee or tea and sit silently before Him for ten minutes. That's right, no phone, no computer, no distractions...just you and Jesus. Don't say a word, just fix your heart on Him, and fill your mind with thoughts about His goodness and love.

~Take a bike ride with God and just talk. Imagine He is riding next to you. If you don't have a bike, walk, climb a tree, or draw away to some place special.

~Choose 5 topics to pray for, such as abortion, world hunger, girls who starve themselves, school shootings and bullying. Your prayers really do make a difference! God is just waiting for someone on earth to agree with His heart. Be the one who stands in the gap!

~Ask God how He is feeling. Ask what's on His heart today! Ask what He loves. Discover what He hates. Ask Him to reveal His thoughts and heart to you.

 ~Speak God's living Word over your life. Pray 5 scripture verses over your life...then believe them!

~Pretend you're planning to teach a Bible Study for your friends. Dig into a passage, and plan the entire lesson. You'll learn so much!

~Listen to your favorite love song. Imagine God is singing it over you!

~Open up and talk to the Lord about something you've never told anyone. Talk about what has hurt you recently. Cry with Him. Be angry. Say whatever you have to. He wants to heal your heart.

~Choose 5 celebrities in Hollywood and pray scripture verses over them.

~Choose to think about one Bible verse ALL DAY LONG. Say it to yourself continually, over, and over, and over again. You'll be amazed at how the Living Word speaks to your heart!

~Talk about your future with God. Plan your dream home, journal about your dream life, and have fun talking with Him about what could be. Ask Him to reveal what He has in store!

~Boldly ask for an assignment in your school. Ask God to lay one person on your heart for you to reach out to every single day, showing the love of Jesus to someone who is lost. Be consistent and stick with that person for six months...praying for their salvation, and being their friend.

Renewing Your Mind With Transforming Power
"Do not conform to the pattern of this world, but be *transformed* by the renewing of your mind. Then you will be able to test and approve what God's will is, His good, pleasing and perfect will." {Romans 12:2}

Do you know what the word *transform* means? It means to change energy from one kind to another, to change an electrical current into one of different voltage.

God desires to give you a new kind of energy. The same energy that lights up the stars at midnight. He wants to infuse you with strength and purity! He wants to transform everything that has been sick and tried, weak and disgusting, into something gloriously new. He wants you to shine like a glow-stick on the beach.

He wants your heart to explode with God's goodness, like fireworks on the Fourth of July. He wants to set you up like dynamite, ready to light up this world for Him!

How does a girl transform and renew her mind with this new kind of voltage called *God's grace*? It comes from the electrical current of the living Word. That's right, it comes from your Bible.

God's Word is like a seed. Sometimes it seems small and maybe even unimportant. But sowing time into reading God's Word is the most vital and world-changing thing you can possibly do. Why? Because it's HIS Words that bring the fire and the power to change this world. You can't change anything on your own, in your human strength.
But with God, and His Word living inside of you, you can do everything!

Girl, everything that you *think* and everything that you *do* has immeasurable potential and power. When you connect with God, clinging to His heart, renewing your mind in His Word, soaking in His presence, asking Him to do all He wishes and surrendering your very self? Woah, look out world. There will be no force that can stop you.

I strongly urge and challenge you not to neglect God's Word. Again, it might seem trivial and unimportant, but only the smallest seeds give birth to the greatest world-changing things! Invest time into the Word, and you will be blown away by what God does in your heart and mind. God's Word can turn your kryptonite into *dynamite*. Don't try to live this life without His Word! Because Jesus *is* the Word.

If you're not sure where to begin, check out these verses, which talk about how there is only one way to transfom our minds from pauper's to princesess, by the Word!

Check out Psalm 1, Romans 12:2, 2 Corinthians 10:3, John 8:32 and Mark 4:24.

Every thought drops a seed,
By God's grace I can lead,
Every rebel thought into captivity,
Down prostrate before the King,
Divine power from the Holy Spirit,
Trust in Him and He will do it,
Help me to use my authority,
To demolish strongholds, lies and crooked things,
Proud weeds that prop themselves up,
Bitterly take root in soil that's puffed up.

But these wild weapons will not remain,
They will not fulfill the purpose for which they came,
I command all thoughts into obedience,
Yielding to Christ and His Spirit alone,
I cast all pride before His throne,
I conform no longer for this mind was made to be,
Constantly renewed, all bitter turned to sweet,
My mental energy is radically changed,
No longer held back with apathetic chains,
By the fruitful flower of Christ in me,

He electrified and birthed many seeds in me.

Seeds of life, joy, beauty and peace;
Seeds of redeption and liberty,
Wash my mind with the water of the Word,
And soon these seeds will be home for the birds,
A place to rest, perch and play,
A mighty fruit tree, prosperous each day,
Intimately connected, intermingled with the Vine,
This garden of God's glory is the garden of my mind.

~*~

Crowning Qualities of a Godly Woman

As Ladies in Waiting, there is a thing or two that we need to learn and grow in before God can ever join us with our Prince. It's vital that during this time we stay in the presence of the King. Because in that place, we will learn all the ways of the Kingdom and how to be a woman after God's own heart. I know there are many crowning qualities, but the Lord gave me these 5 that I hope will be a blessing. When you are born again (John 3:3) and you spend time in the presence of the King, He will always pour even more into your heart and spirit.

1. Virtue:

"Who can find a virtuous woman? For her price is far above rubies." Proverbs 31:10

"A virtuous woman is a crown to her husband." Proverbs 12:4

Virtue – "behavior showing high moral standards of goodness, righteousness, morality, integrity, dignity, honor, decency, nobility, worthiness and purity."

These seem like pretty high standards to live up to, but I love the scripture that says, "I can do ALL THINGS through Christ, which strengthens me." Philippians 4:13

Time in the Word and prayer will help build and strengthen these qualities in your life, as will having a mentor, mother, sister, friend, etc., who walks in these qualities that you can look up to. In my own life, I have been blessed to have a mother that fears the Lord and lives a daily life of example for me. She has been faithful to teach me in all areas, from putting powder and perfume on clean sheets, making pie crust from scratch, knowing how to deep clean a house, the importance of fragrance in a home, and playing worship music which invites the presence of the Lord right in.

Sure, it may sound old fashioned but let me assure you, these are some things that will certainly add to your qualities of virtue and make your house into a home. Husbands do notice and appreciate the little things, by the way.

With God's grace and our diligence, it is possible for each and every one of us to be virtuous women in the world we live in.

This world needs to have examples of women that have a standard of excellence and that conduct themselves with dignity and grace. Amen!

2. A Devotional (Faithful) Spirit:

"The heart of her husband does safely trust in her, so that he shall have no need of spoil (deep concern)." Proverbs 31:11

"A talebearer (a gossip) reveals secrets but he that is of a FAITHFUL spirit conceals (keeps) the matter." Proverbs 11:13

Being trustworthy and faithful are some of the most important attributes a person can have. For a husband to trust his heart and life with his wife, or for friends to trust their deepest secrets with each other is worth more than gold! Many homes, families, friendships, churches, etc. have been destroyed because things were "shared" that were meant to be kept in confidence. It is so important that we learn this Biblical principle at an early age.

I always tell young women: If you can't be faithful in the little things, how can God entrust you with the work of His Kingdom? God can't trust you to be faithful to His people (or the earthly prince he has for you!) when you're untrustworthy with even your own friends and family.

Let us purpose in our hearts to be faithful, first unto the Lord and then to the precious relationships He gives us.

3. A Giving Heart:

"She stretches out her hand to the poor; yea, she reaches forth her hands to the needy." Proverbs 31:20

"The righteous shows mercy and gives." Psalms 37:21

"Give and it shall be given unto you." Luke 6:38

There's a well-known quote that says, "You cannot out give God," and oh how true that is! Giving does not just mean money. The greatest giving comes through laying down our lives for the Lord and for others.

Sisters, you'll never lose by giving. You will never lose by going the second mile! Even the Princesses that we all knew growing up were known for having kind and giving hearts. How much more should we as daughters of the King, be generous and giving, as He has been with us?

I encourage you today to bless someone, to give a gift, a kind note, flowers, a meal, etc. It will bring you much joy, and I assure you that God will bless you in return and meet ALL your needs. Amen!

4. Modesty:

"Strength and Honor are her clothing; and she shall rejoice in time to come." Proverbs 31:25

"In like manner also, that the women adorn themselves in modest apparel, with shamefacedness (shyness) and sobriety. Not with braided hair, or gold, or pearls, or costly array; but with that which becometh women professing godliness."
1 Timothy 2:9-10

Modesty is a very touchy subject these days for young Christian women. I understand that we all have our different convictions, but what I would like to ask young women is this: Whose eye are you really trying to catch? Because the way a woman dresses reveals her true heart and character!

When people look upon you, they should see a reflection of the Lord's grace and beauty. It should draw them to the things of God, not away from.

A lot of men will only be attracted to what they see, to fleshly things. They will lust after flesh, without longing to protect and preserve your purity. The right man who has a heart after God, will encourage you to be modest and will protect the beauty of what God has given you. He will encourage you to be a woman of holiness and purity before the Lord. Let the fear of God and a Godly character determine what you put on.

5. Wisdom:

"She opens her mouth with wisdom and in her tongue is the law of kindness." Proverbs 31:26

"The fear of the Lord is the beginning of wisdom. A good understanding have all they that do His commandments; His praise endures forever." Psalms 111:10

"Out of the abundance of the heart, the mouth speaks." Matthew 12:34

The things that come out of our mouth reveal what's really in our heart. As women of God, we need to constantly ask the Lord to put a guard over our mouth. It's so important to be speaking life into people, our husbands and our children. Not tearing them down. Remember that life and death lies in your tongue!

Yes, we're human, we make mistakes. Sometimes our temper can get the better of us, but it's something that we really need to work on. How can you expect to be in ministry or married if you lash out at people when your soul gets offended?

Like the Proverbs 31 woman, when she opened her mouth, wisdom and kindness came out.

Let us strive to be like that, sisters! Choose life today and choose to have the mannerisms of a Princess. People out there need your encouragement.

Let us purpose in our hearts to have a virtuous spirit like the Proverbs 31 woman, a faithful spirit and a giving heart like Ruth, a modest spirit as women professing Godliness and a heart full of wisdom like Queen Esther.

Love and prayers,
~Kenya-Nicole

~*~

Priceless Princess
An Interview with Joel Smallbone
for KING & COUNTRY

Meet Joel

Joel Smallbone is one of two brothers that make up the band known as *for KING & COUNTRY*. As the brothers of Rebecca St. James, Joel and Luke grew up in the music and ministry scene. Although *for KING & COUNTRY* officially originated in 2011, the brothers and their band go back further than that.

For us, connecting with *for KING & COUNTRY* to feature them in *The Royalty Issue* was kind of a no-brainer. *for KING & COUNTRY* is passionate about telling everyone that they are priceless and unique.

I (Natalee Jensen) had the opportunity to interview Joel, and we kicked the conversation off with a series of silly, light-hearted questions, followed by some serious, thought-provoking ones.

You are a Priceless Princess!

This issue of *Crown of Beauty Magazine* is all about Royalty. Whether we're playfully talking about our favorite Disney Characters like Cinderella, or admiring the characteristics of brave King Arthur, royalty is a very important subject.

Most women feel as if they aren't worth it, like they are anything but royal. Because of this, girls are uninformed of how beautiful and loved they truly are. So these uninformed girls start hanging around others who do not treat them with respect and honor. They are not treated like the true princess they are.

"Luke and I are both recent newlyweds. Luke was married three-and-a-half years ago, and I was married around seven months ago. We grew up in a family with seven of us kids, and one of the greatest lessons that we learned was respect and honor. *for KING & COUNTRY* is all about respect and honor. We believe that respect and honor in relationships is what God intended. We are constantly talking to girls about their worth. They are priceless. Every opportunity that we get, we tell ladies, both young and old, that they are to be respected in relationships. Don't ever settle for second best." –Joel

Take it from a guy who knows. You girls are SO worth it and don't you dare let any boy tell you that you aren't.

"Society seems to suggest for women to talk, dress, act, think, and feel cheap. But we believe that God says that you are priceless." –Joel

The Penny Project
for KING & COUNTRY has not only spoken out about our value as women, but have coupled their words with daunting action! The Smallbone brothers wear necklaces that are the size and color of a one-cent coin. These necklaces have the word PRICELESS stamped into them. These necklaces symbolize the fact that females are worth a lot more than all of the money in the world.

"Who can find a wife of noble character? Her worth is far above rubies!" -Proverbs 31:10

"What is the price of a life? The payment is too high - too costly to count." -Psalm 49:8

"It is incredible. We have literally seen thousands of guys and girls rally behind this cause and wear these necklaces. When women are wearing these necklaces they are saying, 'I know what I am worth; I am a princess and I deserve to be treated like one,' and men are saying, 'We'll step up to the plate. We'll stand out, chivalry is NOT dead; it is time for us to treat these ladies as they are supposed to be treated, with respect and honor.'" –Joel

Joel said almost every night that they have a performance, they see girls walk in and their band members catch a glimpse of the girls' wrists. They can see the cut marks lining their arms. He shared about a girl who came in with a t-shirt rolled up in her hand. She handed it to him and said to read it later. When he got on the bus that night he read the t-shirt. It simply said that on that Monday before, she was planning on ending her life. But the proof of God's love saved her.

"Music is definitely the vehicle for us; we love the music we have a passion for it. And it is moments like with the girl and her t-shirt that you see people respond to the message. They don't respond with a leisurely gesture, they respond in such a radical way that you are very honored to be doing what you are doing." –Joel

Mighty Knights of Valor
It isn't just men who can encourage women to embrace their worth; women have a responsibility to encourage the men they know to become those Prince Charmings and Knights in Shining Armor.

"I sort of feel as though the Prince Charmings and the Knights in Shining Armor are the ones who aren't noticed as much. They are the ones who aren't quite in the limelight. They are the ones that are sincere, outstanding, moral, and thoughtful men. In this day and age, the immediate thing that pops into mind are the visuals, the ones who look dreamy and are all flirtatious. But there is so much more to it than that. Prince Charming is a man who you would see serving the poor and the needy. He would be the one taking care of the widows and the orphans. Someone who would look after their parents. Someone who would serve in a job with his whole heart and soul, no matter what the job is. In my mind, a true Prince Charming is a man who really follows Jesus and His principles in a radical way." –Joel

So how can we encourage these Prince Charmings to really step up and become Godly Knights in Armor?

"There is a scripture that says, 'Whatever is good, whatever is positive, whatever is lovely, whatever is praiseworthy, think about these things.' I think that a lot of men and women these days have lost that sense of chivalry and respect and what it means to truly love someone. I'm talking about love beyond that warm and fuzzy feeling. I am talking about dedication and commitment. The greatest way for women to encourage men to be all that they can be is to do just that. To encourage them. To find the good things and spur them on, but also to find the things that need a little help, and to talk about it with them. Honesty and encouragement is the best way for a woman to encourage a man to be the Prince Charming that they were meant to be." –Joel

True L-O-V-E
Sometimes finding and recognizing true love can be tough.
But, five simple words is enough to realize what true love really is.

"Patience, kindness, self-control, honesty, and thoughtfulness. I pulled off of the Fruits of the Spirit, but they are all good descriptive words of what true love really is." -Joel

In movies and books, we've all obsessed, cried, and sighed over true love. Sometimes true love happens between the super hero and the damsel in distress. Sometimes the girl falls for the super hero because of his super powers, or good looks. But sometimes, it is because of his handsome heart.

"I think that I would choose to be sort of like that Wolverine character. Like if I had the super power of flight, I could fly around and somebody could shoot me down. Or if my super power was super strength, I might be the most fragile person that you have ever met. I would choose Wolverine's powers to save a damsel in distress, because he is strong but not fragile." –Joel

But sometimes those attractive super powers wear off, or he forgets his vow to protect her and has to leave his damsel behind. Sometimes the damsel decides that she is going to do something radical with her life other than sitting in a tower crying out for a super hero to rescue her. Sometimes a girl decides to do the most daring thing. She wipes her tears, lifts up the pen of choice she's been given, and decides to change history with her story. We asked Joel who his favorite heroines are from history?

"I'm not sure that there is one specific thing that a young woman could do to change history. Mary, the mother of Jesus, was an ordinary girl. I think that it was pretty terrific that these angels came to her and started saying these things that no human thought was possible. These angels told Mary that she was going to become pregnant. But she wasn't going to have just an ordinary baby. The child that she would give birth to was going to save the world. And the crazy thing is, Mary was willing; she obviously didn't have a choice, but she was willing anyway." -Joel

His two other favorites?

"Joan of Arc. She stood for something that she believed in."

And, "My mother, her dream ever since being a young girl, was to be married and have a family. That was her passion in life. She raised seven children, two of which are in *for KING & COUNTRY* and the other five are off doing extraordinary things. Her greatest mission was to be a mother."

"My encouragement for the ladies reading this is simple. Ask yourself this question, 'What is something that you are passionate about? What is something that you feel your heart is stirring you to do? What is stopping you, are you afraid? Are you frightened of what others might think of you?' When you pray about it and God makes it clear, pursue that dream with everything in you."

"The two running themes are: Be more interested in standing for something beyond yourself. Stop searching for your own fulfillment and your own happiness, and start searching for others. And no matter what you do, be passionate about it." –Joel

Joel's words are coming from a heart that cares. These words are for every girl out there who is unaware, forgets, or sometimes doubts her beauty, worth, or the love that God has for her. Treasure these words, because they are for you:

"I think that my encouraging words to the beautiful ladies out there would be this: know what you are worth and know who you are. Be-YOU-tiful. The other thing is, no past, no man, or no job can or should ever define who you are. Jesus came to earth to rid you from that, to provide a clean slate. The greatest honor of freedom is embracing that you are a Jesus follower and embracing who Jesus truly is. The things that each of us will face in our lives, there will be only one thing that will help you steady, His name is Jesus. Lean on Jesus. He will redefine your life and give you a freedom that you have never felt." –Joel

There you have it girls!

Believe with your whole being that you are indeed priceless. God designed you perfectly, He didn't randomly choose your hair or your eyes; He made them in the image of Himself. You were made beautifully.

You are precious in God's eyes. You are the daughter of the King! Do you know what that makes you? Being the daughter of the King instantly puts you in the princess category. Always remember, Princess, you are priceless.

Joel's Picks:
Favorite Princess: Thumbelina, mostly because she is the outcast and most people don't think she is worth the time of day; when clearly, she is priceless!

Favorite Foods: Sushi, and raw green beans with pepper and salt.

If you could have afternoon tea with any four Royals, who would you choose: The Queen of England, King Arthur, The Pharaoh (the one in the OT who made Joseph his assistant), and Prince William.

If you could star in any big-screen movie or exciting novel, what type would you choose: An epic plot. Whether a classic adventure like Star Wars or the gory Hunger Games, I would like to play a role in which I could fight for liberty, justice, love, and then ultimately die for a worthy cause. There is not a more profound role than one who selflessly dies for what they believe in.

Fun fact: When *for KING & COUNTRY* was beginning, their producer originally suggested names like The Deep, Joel and Luke, and Austoville. But only one name stuck.

"*'For King and Country!'* was an old English battle cry. They would charge into battle for their king and their country. We thought it was very appropriate for what Luke and I are all about. Ultimately we want to live for our King, Jesus."

~*~

Hidden Diamonds

"Sometimes I think God sprayed me with a huge bottle of boy repellent, just for the fun of it." Ally's quirky comment reminded me of her single status.

My reply was just as single, yet not quite so humorous. "God must think really highly of my future husband, because He hasn't let any boy come near me with a ten-foot pole!" I sighed wistfully, "I hope he appreciates it."

Conversations like this happen every few weeks when I ask Alyssa if she has any secret admirers hiding love notes in her cubby at work, or hunky guys on the block writing her love songs. Her response is always the same, then it's her turn to ask me about my lack of love life. We joke about becoming old, senile cat ladies who will wear polyester pants and date imaginary boyfriends who don't exist.

Choosing not to date was exciting at first. It was rebellious and gutsy. Proudly sporting our *Barlow Girl* T-shirts in middle school was *almost* the cool thing to do. In high school, we joined forces in support of our No Dating Campaign. But now, as many of our friends are inviting us to watch them slow dance with Prince Charming at their weddings, we can't help but glance at one another, and wonder if there's something wrong with us.

Hidden Treasure
Do you ever feel invisible to the guys in your life? Maybe you feel like you're the only girl without a prom date. Sometimes I feel like a weary Rapunzel, locked up in an intimidating tower of stone which keeps my Flynn Rider far, far away.

Sneaky lies pounce on every opportunity of doubt to whisper things like, "You're unattractive. You're a major dork. All your friends have someone special to hold hands with on the Fourth of July. You dream of fireworks, sparks and romance, but you've never even been asked on a date before! You don't get special attention from guys, because you're not worthy of it."

Do these words sound familiar? Lies attempt to disguise themselves in sneaky shades of truth. If we're not careful, we can easily slip into a place of discouragement. Magazines, music, Hollywood, and movie screens tell me that without a guy on my arm I'm painfully pathetic. What good am I if I don't have what it takes to capture his heart? Isn't that what it's all about…beauty?

Sweet sister, don't believe these shadowy words to be true. If we strike a match on the stone of Jesus and light the candle of God's Word, these darkened lies will suddenly be illuminated with a dazzling truth.

In Job, Chapter 28, Job talks about a deep, dark place. He speaks of hidden treasure buried underground. A mine of glorious, priceless jewels are hidden, but the sparkling diamonds resting there are not for the eyes of man. Only God sees "the place where gold is refined." (verse 1).

Verse 10 says, "He tunnels through the rock; His eyes see all its treasures, He searches sources of the rivers, and brings hidden things to light."

My favorite verse in this passage is verse 6, "Sapphires come from its rocks, and its dust contains nuggets of gold."

One might look at these verses and say, "What kind of injustice is this? Why are those lovely pieces of gold, silver, and sapphires forced to live in the dirt where no one can see them? They should be honored and adored, noticed and cherished! Why would God hide them away like that?"

These treasures would only be found by those who would seek them out. God didn't make these treasures obvious and place them on a display table. He knew that lazy men would never dive into the depths of the earth. He knew that only those men who truly desired and valued the treasure would seek it. The men who would humble themselves and be willing to get a little dirty…those are the guys who are forever rewarded with the prize.

The same is true with you. You are beautiful. You're a dazzling diamond. The Bible says that you were woven together in the depths of the earth. Because you are so valuable and lovely, the Lord has hidden you in the shade of His right hand. You're under his covering, and you may feel as though you're locked in a tower. You are tucked away, but not to rot. You've been hidden so that your beautification process can continue, without being tainted by the fingerprints of man. You shine like stars in the universe. You have an expensive price tag on your soul that could only be matched by Someone so priceless as the King of Kings, the Majesty of Heaven, God's only son, Jesus.

Be encouraged sister. God does have a man for you! He won't be a selfish, shallow jerk who only takes what is free and easy. If you stay hidden in God's presence, this man will set out on the greatest adventure of his life as he humbles himself and travels through the deepest places of life…just to find you, his eternal treasure.

Cinderella was hidden for a purpose. A parade of guys didn't pound on her door. Gentlemen callers didn't fill up the parlor. We all know that Cinderella wasn't ugly, socially awkward, or unattractive in any way… she was glorious! She was a Princess, hidden until the perfect time for love to awaken.

Do you remember that magical scene when Cinderella entered the ball room for the first time? Every jaw dropped and Prince Charming stared at this mysterious girl. Who was she? Where had she come from? Charming was suddenly hit with an astonishing realization…he didn't know anything about this girl, but he wanted to know everything. She was like nothing he had ever seen.

Some say Charming fell head over heels because of her sparkly blue dress or luxurious blonde hair, but I believe Charming saw something beyond sparkles and glitter…He saw the defining element, the one thing that set her apart from every other pretty face in the room. He saw a beautiful heart. Patience and kindness were glowing from her eyes. She didn't flaunt and strut into the room…instead she gracefully walked in thankfulness. Her humble heart posture enabled her to be exalted to the high place of Princess. Charming knew that this was his future Queen.

In order to walk in the heavenly splendor of a Princess like Cinderella, we must first allow ourselves to be humbled and changed in the hidden, secret place. Dirt is the place where diamonds are discovered.

Let God use your season of hidden singleness to create something breathtakingly beautiful.

~*~

Prince Spotlight: Prince Phillip

About a month ago, I watched Sleeping Beauty for the first time in years, and it sparked some interesting ideas.

Let's talk about Phillip for a second. He just glows with righteousness. Consider the fact that the fairies actually give him what they call the "Shield of Virtue" and the "Sword of Truth," which he uses not only to fight for his girl, but for the kingdom as well. Phillip not only radiates righteousness like a man of God, but in a way, his actions also reflect Christ.

But this isn't just about the fact that Sleeping Beauty can be seen as an allegory for Christ and the world. I also want to suggest to you that maybe there are men out there like Phillip, reflections of Christ, who will someday fight for you. You deserve nothing less than a champion who will slay as many dragons as he has to, in order to rescue you from your tower. It sounds old-fashioned, I know, but it's incredibly true. There's something in our hearts that desires that; not because we're weak or helpless, but because we want to know that we're worth fighting for.

Please don't misunderstand me—I'm not trying to encourage you to expect perfection from your future prince. That's not possible. But, because you are a princess, I think it's entirely reasonable that you look for a prince. The only perfect Prince, of course, is Christ. He is the ultimate Prince of Peace and Savior of the world, and no mortal man is ever going to be able to compare to that. But here's the good news: That Prince has already saved you and is waiting for you to give him your heart (if you haven't already), and someday, you're going to get to spend eternity by His side in a castle more glorious than any you could imagine. The other good news is this: true men of God can (and should) reflect the nature and actions of Christ. Let me tell you a secret: I don't admire Prince Phillip, and I don't gush about Mr. Darcy or swoon over Aragorn because they're handsome, morally flawless or men idealized by wishful thinking of the female brain. I want a Mr. Darcy, a Prince Phillip, because they resemble my Savior.

Think about this: Let's say we (the earth as a whole, but especially us as individual women) were like Aurora. Just say that maybe some evil power had cast a spell on us (like Maleficent, for example, "Now, shall you deal with me, O Prince, and all the powers of hell!") that maybe we touched something we weren't supposed to touch (we're most certainly not perfect, either) and fell into a deep, shadowy slumber. And then let's say there was also a prince, like Phillip. And maybe that Prince was determined to save the love of his life, his true bride, however lost she was. So he jumped unhesitatingly, courageously, mightily into the fray. Maybe the righteousness of that Prince conquered the powers of evil, and with his kiss, he woke his bride up again; let the light back into her eyes and slashed away the thorns that were encroaching on her heart. Do you understand what I'm getting at? Doesn't it make your heart thrill? Christ is our prince, and He did exactly that for us.

In this lifetime, I'm never going to see Jesus Christ face to face. I won't get to speak with Him and actually see Him and hear Him until I get to that eternal kingdom someday. Until then, however, I can look at the children of God in the world around me, and I can see reflections of His face and hear echoes of His voice in them. That's one of the most wonderful things about the body of Christ—we all get to be little, fragmented glimpses of Heaven or scraps of conversation from the throne room of God for our fellow Christians.

And that's also what "true love" and marriage according to God's plan are about. They're a representation of the relationship between Christ and His church, His bride. Every marriage or relationship that's leading towards marriage is supposed to be just that—which means that you are definitely a Princess, and that your future husband should most definitely be a Prince.

So guess what, girls? You know how you've always wanted to be a Disney Princess in a fairytale? Well, you're going to get something even better—you're a Princess of God in reality, and right this minute God's picking out the perfect guy to be your leading man.

~*~

About the Author:
Noelle Hilpert is attending Berea College . She was home schooled up until college and is a pastor's kid. When she was eight years old, she decided that she wanted to be a writer, and has been penning stories, poems, and occasionally songs ever since, all which led to a major in Creative Writing. She loves girly things like Disney and Taylor Swift, but is also a lit nerd and has a slight (by which huge is meant) obsession with science fiction and British television. Most importantly, she is a Daughter of the King, who hopes to help others come into their inheritance as the children of God.

The Season of Cinderella

You know those seasons in life where it seems like just about everything that could possibly go wrong, does? Those seasons where challenges and heartache abound, and it feels like no one is cheering you on, letting you know that things are going to be okay?

I like to call that, the season of Cinderella, Part 1. (Because we all know that Cinderella, Part 2 is amazing!) But when you're stuck in the depressing scene in Cinderella's story, where the evil step Mom has the upper hand, the glass slipper is broken, and you're locked in the tower. Hope for a happily ever after seems far off.

We can take courage and comfort in the fact that every heroine who has gone before us, has been in a season just like this. Our favorite ladies in the Bible were all faced with the same choice that we have today.

Are we going to live in the flesh, and believe the deceptive mirage that that enemy has set up all around us? Are we going to adapt to the temporary scenery of trials and think, "Well, I guess this is as good as it gets. I'm always going to be broken and disappointed."? Or are we going to do what the Bible implores us to do, and live in the Spirit? Will we choose to align with Heaven, think God's thoughts, speak His Words, and worship Him no matter what's going on around us?

Paul made it very clear in Romans, Chapter 8:
"For to be carnally minded is death, but to be spiritually minded is life and peace." {Verse 6.}

We cannot fix our thoughts on the temporary situation of what's happening on this earth. Because in a few short moments everything will change. Reality will hit. Everything that has been hidden will be revealed. Hearts will be uncovered, and motives exposed. When the final curtain drops on this drama called life, we will all appear before the judgment seat of Christ.

Our lives will be tested through the blazing fire of His glory, and only what is pure will remain. Only what is in Christ will remain. Only absolute goodness, purity, and love will endure. Everything else will be done away with, and completely consumed by flames. And in that moment your true self will be revealed.

When Jesus appears, we the Bride of Christ will appear. It's hard to imagine what that day will be like. But whenever I find myself day dreaming about the glorious unfolding of Heaven, my mind drifts to the story of Cinderella. In the 2015 live-action Disney version of this tale, I envision the scene where Cinderella's dreams finally come true, and her pumpkin carriage carries her to the castle where the Prince lives. She enters the stunning castle wearing a most glorious gown. As the Prince's eyes meet hers, it is as if time stands still. He takes her hand, and leads her into a mesmerizing waltz.

When we finally see Jesus face-to-face, that moment is going to be ten-trillion times more beautiful than anything Hollywood could dream up. I believe that even the angels will gasp in wonderment when the Bride's true nature is unveiled, for she has been tenderly created in the very image of Christ.

We will be clothed in the most breath-taking garments of righteousness, far more gorgeous than Cinderella's gown. The righteousness that we will wear will be so stunning, because it is the VERY beauty and glory of God! God will bestow His beauty upon us, and our hearts will sparkle like dazzling diamonds.

For the first time in forever, our inside will become our outside, and the true nature of our character will be revealed. The life we lived will be the garments we wear. The worship we poured out upon Jesus will be the jewels that He places in our crowns.

Just like in Cinderella's world, everything will suddenly be flipped inside out. Her inner beauty - her kindness and faithful, steadfast love - was never noticed, applauded or appreciated. Those around her took advantage of her; they bullied, betrayed, and persecuted her tender soul.

But in the blink of an eye, everything changed. Her tears were transformed into diamonds. Her ashes into beauty.

The girl who sat by the cinders of broken dreams, was swept up by a tidal wave of joy, totally overtaken by the goodness of her Prince. He redeemed everything. He swept her away into her happily ever after, placed a crown of glory upon her head, and declared her to be His queen!

Sister, you should rejoice in the fact that you find yourself in a Cinderella season, because after times of trial, unspeakable JOY is coming. This is your happily ever after! This is your reality! As God's royal ones, we have so much to look forward to. We must lock our hearts on this reality:

You have an address in Heaven. This is not your home. Everything that you see now IS going to pass away. Only what is unseen is eternal. The Lord is going to lavish His love and goodness upon you in ways that you never even DREAMED possible. Heaven will take your breath away. His overwhelming presence will cause you to forget every terrible, painful memory.

The price of denying yourself, carrying your cross, and following after Him will all be worth it. Every tear. Every sacrifice. Every battle. It will suddenly seem so trivial and insignificant, when the waves of His love crash over your soul!

Those who walked before us had to learn the secret of living in the Spirit, setting their hearts on Heaven, and so do we. If they didn't, discouragement would have struck them down and left them paralyzed by fear. Take a moment to think of the ladies in the Word who lived in a Cinderella season.

Sarah was barren and dreamed of having a son more than anything. Ruth lost her husband. Esther was ripped away from her home, and forced to live in the palace of a pagan King. Hannah was heartbroken when she couldn't conceive. And Mary was asked to do just about the craziest thing ever heard of! Carry the Son of God in her virgin womb!

But what did these women do? They "judged Him faithful who had promised" {Hebrews 11:11}, and "entrusted themselves to the One who judges justly!" {1 Peter 2:23}

In the world's eyes, these ladies looked like total losers. Pathetic, heartbroken, hopeless Cinderellas. But look what glorious endings of triumph they had! And because of their sacrifices and Godly examples, we are encouraged by their stories. Why? Because we know the ending.

Well guess what. I know the ending of your story too! You are a co-heir with Christ. In Heaven you will rule and reign with Him. You will make some HUGE decisions. You will advance the Kingdom. You will walk in the fullness of your true self, and will never doubt or question your royal identity.

But what about right now, while we are on this earth? If all of this is true, and we have a royal calling, royal influence, and royal authority, then why aren't we walking in it? Why are we waiting for Heaven to be who we truly are?

I don't know about you, but I don't want to be surprised when I get to Heaven and see a crown upon my head. I don't want to look at the signet ring of authority upon my finger, the royal robe on my back, and the smile upon my Daddy's face, and think, "What?! You mean this is who I was all along!? Beautiful, kind, gracious, powerful, influential, loving, and regal? I had the same calling of Esther upon my life, to speak up for those who cannot speak for themselves, to dine with kings and people of great influence, to love the un-lovable and inspire those around me to greatness, and I DIDN'T do anything about it?! I had all of Heaven backing me up, just waiting to answer my prayers, and I didn't ASK for the impossible?! The angel armies of Heaven were just waiting for me to lift my voice and cry out against injustice, and I didn't DO anything?!"

For many, the life that we live in Heaven will be such a shocking revelation. So many Christians live their lives without knowing who they are in Christ. But I don't want to wait until Heaven to be who I was created to be.

I want to receive as much revelation as possible while I am on this earth, about who my Daddy is, who Jesus is, who the Holy Spirit is, and who I am! I wasn't raised in a palace, and don't understand the way God's Kingdom, royal rules, Heavenly economy, and monarchy authority work, therefore I must seek the Lord and cry out for Him to reveal this reality. How will a Princess ever know how to behave in the courts of the King, if she doesn't spend any time with Him?

I am a citizen of Heaven, growing up in America. I won't know how to live, and act, and BE according to my Daddy's Kingdom, if I don't actively seek Him! How will I know what to do, or what to say, if I don't see my Heavenly Father move and speak? I need the Holy Spirit to daily reveal everything I need to know! He is my teacher!

Princess, we are on this journey together. Even Queen Esther had to have her mind renewed in the presence of royalty, before she could walk in her calling as Queen. She was required to undergo a whole year's worth of beauty treatments. The same is true for us. If we want to walk in the royal reality of who we are, we must spend time with our King, and allow Him to transform and renew everything about us!

And today, we need to entrust our hearts and souls once again to the One who loves us so dearly and tenderly. Just like Cinderella, we must believe that He is writing out our beautiful ending.

A scene that I so adore in the Cinderella movie is at the climax when it appears that all hope is lost. Yet she is still singing. She opens her mouth, and lets a song come from her soul. She once again chooses to believe that things are going to be okay. She remembers the night of dancing with her prince and she can't help but smile and sing. As the song rises, everything begins to change. The mice and birds hasten to her rescue, and open the window so that her prince can hear the song where he is waiting down below.

And just like that, the lies of the evil Step Mother are exposed. Truth is revealed, the wrongs are made right, and justice prevails!

Sister, the same thing happens for us when we choose to lift our voice and sing to the Lord! When we entrust ourselves to the One who judges justly and consider Him faithful who has promised, no matter how foolish or silly we look to the world, the Lord works on our behalf! He is enthroned in our praises, and swiftly comes to our aid!

Royal One, you have such a high calling. Don't allow the enemy to distract you with meaningless, fleshly drama and mind games. Don't listen to the voice of fear. Choose to fix your eyes on the unseen, rather than the seen. Fix your eyes on your King!

You've been sent out by Jesus, on mission impossible, to make disciples of all nations, loving everyone you come in contact with, forcefully advancing His Kingdom of Love.

There is a broken world out there, just aching and waiting for a princess to come and introduce herself to her Prince. You are a minister of peace and reconciliation, an ambassador of Heaven!

It is my prayer that we, as ambassadors, do not represent the wrong nation. I pray that we do not present our royal Kingdom as selfish, materialistic, beauty-saturated, entertainment-binging, food-obsessed, scared, wimpy, depressed, lazy people. We cannot possibly change this worldly culture if we live, think, and act just like it. Sons and Daughters of the King are to be so contrastingly different, that it causes people around us to say, "What do they have that I don't? What planet are they from?"

It is my prayer that we dare to seek our King like never before, and truly get ahold of His heart. That His goodness, glory, and holiness will wash over us and renew our minds. That our spirits would sparkle afresh, as we catch a glimpse of our Heavenly home.

I pray that great courage and daring hope would burst from our souls! I pray that we would love like Jesus does, give so courageously and benevolently, refuse to conform, be undercover agents of change, transform this culture, stand firm 'til the end, and walk in the confidence that we are so DEARLY loved by our King!

Cinderella, you have been promised a beautiful ending. But what are you going to do with the time you've been given? Just like Esther, you have been called to the Kingdom for such a time as this.

So make it your aim to choose once again to walk in the Spirit. To believe that you are seated in heavenly places with Christ Jesus. To stand fast, and no matter what, always choose faith. Laugh at the days to come. Smile because you know the Lord is working it all out for your good, and His glory!

"Stand fast therefore in the liberty by which Christ has set us free, and do not be entangled again with a yoke of bondage."
~Galatians 5:11

~*~

Proverbs 31: Unlocking the Treasure Trove

Reading Proverbs 31 is like opening up a treasure box. Dazzling, "out-of-this-world" wisdom sparkles like necklaces with which we can adorn ourselves. As God's girls, it's an open invitation to dive into this chapter and apply it to our lives. The well of His Word goes so deep, and when we take time to meditate on this chapter we can get lots of revelation! Here are some thoughts about the first few verses...

"Who can find a virtuous wife? For her worth is far above rubies."

When Jesus stretched His arms wide on the cross, and bled and died for us, He loudly proclaimed our worth. Sister, you are *priceless*. Before the cross, we were sinful, ugly, wretched, and ashamed...but He has bestowed upon us His beauty and His value. Now we are royalty! This is mind blowing! We are worth more than rubies, sapphires, gold, or anything of value in this world. Jesus said if a man trades his soul for the entire net-worth of this world, he would make a terrible trade.

Just for fun, I grabbed my calculator and added up the net worth of some of the world's richest people. Just how much money was Jesus talking about? Once I got up to 74-billion-dollars, I was so amazed. Jesus said if we were to trade our soul for 74-billion-dollars, we would get totally ripped off...because each of us is worth more than 74-billion-dollars!

The price tag on my soul is so costly that no one could match it or surpass it...except for the Darling of Heaven, the Son of God! We don't need anyone or anything in this world to give us our value. We are already so, so priceless.

"The heart of her husband safely trusts her, so he will have no lack of gain."

Our Maker has proudly called Himself our husband (Isaiah 54:5). After making such a huge investment in us (the very blood of Jesus!) you'd think He'd be a little nervous about how we're going to make Him look. How will we affect His Name and the glory of His Kingdom?

It says here that He will have no lack of gain. The investment that He has made in us, the Seed of His Word, the Seed of Christ, will produce life and fruit! His love will multiply itself through us if we remain humble and hungry! I don't want to be a selfish princess bride who consumes and spends up the glorious riches of His grace, thinking the world revolves around "mwah!" I want to be a princess bride who is willing to become pregnant with the things of God, letting patience and endurance have its perfect work in my life, sharing in the fellowship of His sufferings, and giving birth to nothing but love.

I want to be a fruitful bride and a co-laborer with Christ. I want Him to trust me and share His secrets with me! "The secret of the Lord is with those who fear Him." {Psalm 25:14}

I desire to be a good and faithful steward of what He has entrusted to me. I want to be obedient to His great commission and live a life worthy of my royal position. Jesus paid much, much too high a price for me to waste His blood in selfishness and apathy! "She does him good and not evil, all the days of her life."

"She seeks wool and flax, and willingly works with her hands."

Being a fruitful bride is not an automatic thing. God said, "You will seek Me and find Me when you seek Me with all of your heart." {Jeremiah 29:13}

Seeking takes effort. Opening our Bibles, opening our hearts, praying, worshiping, and spending time with the Lord takes effort. We can't do it just when we "feel" like it. We must willingly spend our energy on Him. The reward is so, so great. When we find Him, the prize is far greater than anything that we may have to "sacrifice" or give up, in order to gain the precious prize of fellowship with Jesus!

"She is like the merchant ships, she brings her food from afar."

I like to imagine regal ships with big fluffy white sails, gliding across the universe in the Spiritual Realm, bringing everything that I need to live out "mission impossible" (being His princess bride). He has promised to give me everything I need for life and godliness. (2 Peter 1:3) He will provide for all of my needs, according to His riches in glory. He is the King of Heaven! He is the answer to every problem and every need. As citizens of Heaven, it is our privilege and responsibility to bring answers to this earth, using Heaven's resources.

When we dive in and dine on the Word of God, enjoying the banquet table of truth that is set before us...we are bringing exotic foods, spices, and treasures from a faraway land. All the way from Heaven! The world will marvel, and wonder where such beauty, wisdom, and virtue comes from...and we can proclaim that it all comes from our King!

"She considers a field and buys it; from her profits she plants a vineyard."

I see two things in this verse. First of all, it reminds me of the parable Jesus told about the man who found a treasure in a field. After he found it, he sold everything so that he could buy that field. "So it is with the Kingdom of Heaven," Jesus explained. "Once you encounter the King, you will happily give up everything, to have all of me!"

When we catch glimpses of just how amazingly beautiful and worthy our King Jesus is, it puts our whole life in perspective. All of a sudden, those things that hurt and were so unbearable, don't sting quite so badly anymore. When we suffer persecution, or rejection and betrayal from a friend, we remember the One who suffered the ultimate blow. When we're lonely, we remember the One who stepped down from Heaven, left His Perfect Father, and lived in this broken world. When we're exhausted and weary, we remember the One who promised that His strength would be our own. When we think about who He is, and how dearly He loves us, obedience and surrender doesn't look so radical anymore. In fact, it looks quite reasonable!

"I beseech you therefore, brethren, by the mercies of God, that ye present your bodies a living sacrifice, holy, acceptable unto God, which is your reasonable service." {Romans 12:1}

Secondly, we see that the Proverbs 31 woman has guts. She knows how to make decisions. She considers a field, and boom, she buys it. She makes a move. She steps out in faith. She plants a vineyard, bears fruit, and makes a difference in this world.

We, as God's daughters, cannot let fear stop us from moving forward. When His Spirit is leading us to make a move, let's do it. No fear. No hesitation. Just total boldness and obedience. Proverbs says that the righteous are bold as a lion. The Proverbs 31 woman is fierce.

"She girds herself with strength, she strengthens her arms."

Sisters, if you only get one thing out of this entire passage, get this: we are living in a time on this earth, where we must be prepared for what is coming. We are truly living in the last days, and things are bound to get a little bit (or a lotta' bit!) crazy. We must gird ourselves with strength, press into Jesus, spend lots and lots of time in His Word, and in His presence. We must strengthen our arms, our faith, for the days ahead.

I really encourage you to make it priority to spend more time with the Lord than you ever have before! When we do, He trains our hands for battle (Psalm 144:1) and equips us for what is ahead.

"She perceives that her merchandise is good, and her lamp does not go out by night. She stretches her hands to the distaff, and her hand holds the spindle."

This is truly a woman who knows how to get things done. She has a spirit of diligence, not laziness. She doesn't have a slave master, telling her what to do, nagging on her to get things done. She simply sees a need, knows she has the answer and resources from Heaven and does it. Sister, if there is something stirring in your heart, a business you feel the Lord wants you to start, a Bible study He wants you to initiate, a friend whom He wants you to tell about Jesus...then just do it! Take that first step forward, and then be persistent.

As daughters of the King, we must harbor an unstoppable determination deep in our spirits. We must have the tenacity of a bull dog that will not let go until the job is done! Just hold your hand to the spindle and keep it there until it is time to let go!

"She is not afraid of snow for her household, for all her household is clothed with scarlet. She makes tapestry for herself; her clothing is linen and purple."

As girls, we spend plenty of time getting ready in the morning. Hair, makeup, and choosing a totally adorable outfit. But what are we daily dressing our hearts with? How much time do we spend washing and grooming the inside?

It is my prayer that we will wrap ourselves with the truth of our royal identity. Just like Esther put on her royal robes, let's fill our minds and hearts with the truth of who Jesus is, and who we are in His eyes. We are washed with the water of His word, dressed in robes of righteousness, clothed in the scarlet blood of Jesus Christ, and royal clothing of love.

~*~

The Thoughts He Thinks

"For I know the thoughts that I think toward you, says the Lord, thoughts of peace and not of evil..." {Jeremiah 29:11}

The thoughts that God thinks towards us. What are those thoughts? How many thoughts run through His mind every single day, about you?

Not thoughts about your Mom, your sister, or your youth leader.

Thoughts about *you*.

Not thoughts about world peace, or starving children, or presidential elections...thoughts about *just you*.

How much time does God spend thinking about you?

What does He think as you crawl out of bed and pour yourself a cup of coffee? What does He think about your dreams and desires? What does He think about your fears and failures? What is He thinking when you throw your head back and laugh with your friends, or when you feel utterly alone and cry yourself to sleep?

What is He Thinking About You *Right Now*?
"How precious to me are your thoughts O God, if I were to count them, they would outnumber the grains of the sand." {Psalm 139:17}

God is *always* thinking about you. His thoughts concerning you pile up like grains of sand on the seashore. It's unfathomable. We cannot number them. He's been thinking about you since long before you were even born.

We should be excited about this! Why? Because the thoughts He thinks towards us are GOOD thoughts. Thoughts of peace and not of evil. Thoughts full of hope, love, joy, and goodness.

So what is He thinking about you *right now*?

I can tell you what he's not thinking. He's not mad at you. He's not keeping a long record of your past sins and failures. He isn't disappointed. He isn't shaking his head, wondering, "When is she ever going to get this?"

He isn't tired of you. He isn't bored with you. He isn't irritated or exhausted by you.

You are His glorious one in whom is all His delight! He is joyful and excited about your life. Every single second, His love is crashing over you like a tidal wave.

Right now He is thinking, "That's my girl. I love her so much. Oh my goodness, she makes my heart smile. Is she not adorable? I love the uniqueness that I have placed inside of her. Just look at who I have created her to be! Look at her simple obedience. Look at her desire to love Me and know Me. Oh! Did you see that? She is reaching for Me. She is dependent on Me. She is weak and broken and messy and easily discouraged. She thinks she's missing it, but she's not. She's still reaching for Me! She's still seeking Me. So weak, but that means I can be SO strong in her! She is beyond beautiful. Oh how I long for her to see herself through My eyes. She makes Me so excited! She is My favorite creation. She is My daughter, My princess, My lovely one. I have so many great plans for her. I want to tell her about them! I want to talk to her. I want to share My secrets with her. I am ready. I am not holding anything back from her. I am waiting for her to talk to Me. I'm ready for her to seek Me. I am running after her...I want her to turn and run into Me! I love fighting for her! I love being strong and valiant on her behalf! I am the Captain of the Angel Armies, the God who breathed out the stars, and I am on her side! All of heaven is behind her righteous cause! I am for her; I am *not* against her. Awake, daughter, to this truth! Rise up and be all that I have created you to be! I am so beyond excited for you; I love you so much! All you have to do is ask for My Holy Spirit to reveal this love. It's always real. It's always here. I'm always thinking beautiful, amazing, spectacular thoughts of goodness about you."

You might be thinking, "Well that's lovely, but I don't feel like God is actually thinking those things about me. There is so much negativity going on in my head, I have trouble believing those things to be true."

Sister, you must remember that we are not "feelers" we are "believers"! It doesn't matter how you feel. God's truth NEVER changes. Just because we don't experience the reality of His ocean of love crashing over us every second of the day doesn't mean those waves stop coming. He is always POWERFULLY pursuing us and speaking. He is always reaching in our direction. All we have to do is reach back and ask, "God, what are you thinking about me? I want to experience your truth for real! Reveal the truth of Your love!"

The enemy tells us lies about God's thoughts. But the Word of God tells us the truth. The best way to align ourselves with His truth is by immersing ourselves in His Word, and speaking it over our lives.

"And David was greatly distressed, for the people spoke of stoning him...but David encouraged himself in the Lord."{1 Samuel 30:6}

We must encourage ourselves in the Lord. When we speak His words, sing His songs of truth, and refuse to submit to our feelings of abandonment, rejection and fear, we disarm the enemy and give the victory to God.

"So then brothers and sisters, stand firm..." {2 Thessalonians 2:15}

Stand firm, and hold onto the thoughts God thinks towards you. They are Spirit and they are Truth. Nobody can ever change the reality of how God feels about you. Jesus poured out His blood on the cross, and if you have crowned Him as your Savior, you are in a blood covenant with Him. God is not a man that He would lie or change His mind. He doesn't make decisions based on wishy-washy feelings. He is always pure, always noble, always fighting for you, always rejoicing over you, always thinking the best of you, and always calling you upward into the fullness of who He's made you to be.

"Though the mountains be shaken, and the hills be removed, yet my unfailing love for you will NOT BE SHAKEN." {Isaiah 54:10}

Stand firm then, in His unshakable love. The thoughts He thinks toward you truly do outnumber the sands on the seashore. And they are thoughts to prosper you and not to harm you. Thoughts to give you a hope and a future.

~*~

Princess on a Mission

What if I told you that you have been created, chosen, and commissioned to go change this world as we know it? "Change the world" is such a cliché phrase that we hear tossed around in church, on TV, in girl power pop-anthems, and on social media accounts. It has a certain ring to it. But if we're honest, we've heard these words so much that our hearts have become slightly desensitized to the sheer thrill of the raging battle cry behind them.

I am about to hand you a secret strategy that will enable you to powerfully penetrate the evil in this world. This strategy is so simple it can be tempting to say, "That's it? I don't get it. What's so powerful about this?"

"Your beauty should not come from outward adornment, such as elaborate hairstyles and the wearing of gold jewelry or fine clothes. Rather, it should be that of your inner self, the unfading beauty of a gentle and quiet spirit, which is of great worth in God's sight." {1 Peter 3:3}

This is not the kind of beauty that is being celebrated in the earth today. Tragically, most magazine covers and TV shows do not celebrate women of virtue. In our Hollywood-saturated culture, we choose who is celebrated. We crown them as queens and dub them "celebrities." Trendy outfits, catchy pop-songs, and push-up bras...that's what is being celebrated.

Meanwhile, our little-sister generation is attempting to emulate these highly celebrated figures of pop-royalty. They want to wear the same clothes as them, sing their songs, and act like they do.

We've all seen this kind of behavior coming from the little girls in our lives. Whether they are obsessed with Hannah Montana, or Queen Elsa from Disney's "Frozen," little girls love to copy what they see in the older women around them! This is a totally natural, God-given desire in little ones. In fact, Titus 2 instructs the "older women, [to] teach the younger women."

Little girls are more than eager and ready to learn. They desire to become what they see being displayed and celebrated around them. This can be a wonderful thing, but this can also be a bit of a nightmare.
Who is telling these girls what is beautiful? Who decides who will be celebrated and what "cool" is?

I used to be one of those wide-eyed little girls, striving to become like my "cool big sisters" in Hollywood. I can only imagine how much I freaked out my poor Mother when I came running out into the living room as an 8-year-old with my t-shirt rolled up, showing off my belly button, and preppy pig-tails in my hair. I wiggled my hips around and said, "Look Mama! I'm Brittany Spears!

Little girls just want to be like their babysitters, their cool big sisters, and the teen-pop icons they see on TV. Sadly, the "babysitters" on TV and in the media are teaching our little sisters what being a girl is all about...and these messages are advancing the kingdom of Satan...not the Kingdom of God!

In 1 Peter, Chapter 3, the Holy Spirit reveals the powerful secrets to us of His Kingdom strategy in this hour...it shows us what we can do to be PRO-active and how to counteract the devil's twisted scheme. God does not desire for our little sisters to be sucked into this selfish, boy-obsessed, cruel, lying, manipulating culture. Thankfully, there is a flip-side to every coin! In the same way that little girls want to run around and emulate their favorite girls on TV, they also desire to emulate us.

That's right...I'm talking about you! Imperfect you. Messy hair, acne, battle scars, and all!

You, as a princess, have been entrusted with an incredible sphere of influence. Of course, the enemy would desire to blind you to not realize just how great an influence you have on those around you.

But just like Eve, you've been given a garden, a place of influence that is yours to cherish and maintain and be responsible for. It is your job to make sure the serpent of deception stays OUT of your garden. Don't let the cunning snake mess with your sisters! Our battle plan is simply this: Submitting ourselves to everything God is, everything His heart stands for, and everything He has created us to be, then resisting the enemy and foiling his wicked plans. ("Submit to God, resist the devil, and he will flee from you." James 4:7)

The strategy of 1 Peter 3:3 is just like what Jesus did when He came to this earth. He dressed Himself in the garments of humility and did things so backwards and upside down! He positioned Himself to be the exact opposite of everything this world is all about.

The world says a woman's beauty comes from the outside. God says it comes from the inside.

The world says a woman's utmost concern should be looking out for herself. God says her highest concern should be living selflessly, defending and protecting, uplifting and cherishing those around her. The world says a woman's power is in her physical features. God says it is in her humility, when she "entrusts herself to the one who judges justly."{1 Peter 2:23}

The world will consume. We will give.

The world will be jealous and tear apart their sisters. We will build one another up in love.

The world will say it's so hopeless. We will say saving one life is totally worth it.

The world says to freak out and worry. We only have absolute peace.

The world says to take matters concerning "finding true love" into our own hands and push to make something happen. We only wait for God's perfect timing.

The world says one human is worth less than another. We will declare that each life was worth the blood of Jesus.

This pattern of backwards, upside down, inside out living is like swimming upstream. It is not easy. But when we submit to God, declare His Words and His ways to be true as gold, setting an example for our little sisters, it is just like what Jesus did. It is the secret weapon of humility. If we can do this, we will be like dynamite in the hand of our God! Like small stones in the sling of David, the ugly giant will come down.

Princess Sisters, we must learn the secret and walk in the unfathomable power of being faithful and obedient in small, seemingly insignificant things. These things might be some of which the world will laugh and scoff at...but these little droplets of rain will suddenly create a storm! 1 Peter 3:5 continues, "For this is the way the holy women of the past who put their hope in God used to adorn themselves. They submitted themselves to their own husbands, like Sarah, who obeyed Abraham and called him her lord. You are her daughters if you do what is right and do not give way to fear."

Isn't that interesting, that Peter stresses, "do not give way to fear." Why? Because this kind of 1 Peter 3:3 Princess-Living doesn't work if our knees collapse in fear.

So many young ladies conform to the world's idea of what a strong, powerful, beautiful woman is...because they are afraid of entrusting themselves to God and living with such silly, carefree, childlike faith.

Sometimes we act out of fear and insecurity thinking, "If I wait, I will never find my Prince Charming...I'm getting old. I need to make it happen. I need to help him along, I need to give him a hint. I need to wear more revealing clothes so I get more attention."

Or we battle thoughts like this:

I need to ignore the smelly kid by the trash cans, because I might lose some good friendships if they see me with him.

I need to buy myself a new pair of jeans, instead of feeding a child in Africa, because I'll look so uncool if I only have three pairs, when all my friends have like twenty.

I need to do what my parents want me to do with my life, instead of following my God-given dreams, because I'm so afraid of what might happen.

I can't witness to my friends, because they might hate me.

I can't wear a modest bathing suit to the pool, because my friends will laugh at me.

I just can't wait for my future husband, because I feel like he's never coming.

I can't NOT worry about this thing, because it seems so irresponsible!

I can't trade my Saturday night with my girls to read the Word and be alone with God, because that's the only "me" time I have all week.

What do these words sound like? F-E-A-R.

The princess mindset is total abandonment of the world's ways and believing that He, whose name is Faithful and True, is going to write out a beautiful love story for you. Don't let fear and insecurity push you out of the palace. Keep your ground!

I envision this secret, quiet, backwards, princess living to be a lot like what happened in *The Chronicles of Narnia: Prince Caspian.*

Aslan, the powerful lion, gave Lucy a little dagger. She gasped and said, "I don't know if I'd ever be brave enough to use it." It was a small tool, really, maybe enough to kill a mouse, but certainly not an army of bad guys who came storming toward her on horseback. But little Lucy reached for her dagger, and held it out, as if it was a powerful weapon.

The men came barreling forward, hoof-beats pounding. She cringed, wanting to run, thinking about what might happen if the dagger doesn't work. What if the men run her over? She was so, so tiny.

But suddenly, at the most critical moment, Aslan came flying into action. His love saved the day. Aslan devoured them in the blink of an eye. Suddenly, the danger was no more. I think of little Lucy, and how silly and nonsensical she looked, holding out her dagger even though a battle was raging around her.

That's what it looks like for us being 1 Peter 3:3 girls...people will roll their eyes and say, "How are you going to change the world by following God's ways? Dressing modestly? Choosing not to date? Submitting to your God? Choosing not to worry? What's that going to do?"

Sister, do not listen to those voices. Simply hold out your dagger of faith and purity and say, "The Lord will perfect that which concerns me." {Psalm 138:8}

Princess, hold fast and steady...you never know how many little eyes are watching you in awestruck wonderment thinking, "Wow. She is so beautiful. She loves God so much...I want to be just like her someday."

~*~

PART 3: BOYS

QUIZ! Which Disney Dream Dude is Right for You?

Circle the answers that you relate to the most, then tally up your score at the end!

1. Your parents are planning a trip to Disney World! What are you most excited about doing at the Magic Kingdom?

A. Watch fireworks explode at the Cinderella Castle. How whimsical and romantic!

B. Space Mountain! The exhilarating rides are what make the park fun.

C. I would rather go to Sea World instead.

D. The Magic Carpet Ride. Take me on all the kiddy rides. I can't handle anything too crazy.

E. The food. I'll hang out at my favorite ice-cream shop, sit on a bench, and watch for cute boys.

F. Watching the characters interact and perform onstage, that has to be the most fun.

2. Which words best describe the guy you last had a crush on?

A. Blonde hair, blue eyes, perfect smile.

B. Funny, charismatic, and always makes you laugh.

C. Serious and sensitive, with brown eyes and a kind heart.

D. Quiet and mysterious.

E. Confident, adorable, and a little bit cocky.

F. Loves to argue with you, always wants to be right, and drives you a little bit crazy.

3. Which classic Disney song are you always singing?

A. *A Dream Is a Wish Your Heart Makes* from Cinderella

B. *Hakuna Matata* from the Lion King

C. *The Start of Something New* from High School Musical

D. *A Whole New World* from Aladdin

E. *What Dreams Are Made Of* from the Lizzie McGuire Movie

F. *Tale as Old as Time* from Beauty and the Beast

4. Movie night! What are you watching?

A. *Pride and Prejudice.* I love the romantic way of speaking, dancing, and the handsome men!

B. *The Avengers.* I choose all action, all the time.

C. *Star Wars.* Nothing like some classic adventure and sci-fi!

D. *The Hunger Games.* Suspense. Romance. Josh Hutcherson. End of story.

E. *Finding Nemo.* I love animated Disney movies. Just keep swimming, just keep swimming...

F. *Princess Diaries.* Me, a Princess? Why, yes I am!

5. If you could date one of the following dudes in Hollywood, who would you choose?

A. Josh Hutcherson. He's sweet, charming, sensible, and oh so cute.

B. Zac Efron. The handsome boy next door.

C. Harry Styles. Beautiful eyes for the win.

D. Joe Jonas. Tall, dark and handsome. What more could a girl ask for?

E. Louis Tomilson. He's cute, quirky, and always goofing off.

F. Taylor Lautner. He doubles as a werewolf!

6) What is your dream date?

A. A romantic, candle lit dinner at a fancy restaurant, followed by an extravagant fireworks display.

B. An exciting horseback ride. We would get a chance to talk, and then race!

C. Swimming with dolphins. What could be more fun than that?

D. Skydiving. Ahhhhhhhhhh!

E. An ice-cream date. We would explore our favorite shops downtown, then gallivant through the toy-store.

F. A sweet afternoon picnic in the park, with quiet time to read and watch the waves.

7. Take a snapshot! How do you picture your life 10 years from now?

A. Happily married, in a beautiful home, standing by my husband with one son and one daughter.

B. Married, living on a large farm with my amazing man, raising a van full of kids.

C. It doesn't matter, just as long as I'm doing something I love with the people I love.

D. Doing ministry alongside my husband, traveling the world, encouraging and uplifting him to be anyone he wants to be.

E. On stage performing! (Hopefully getting chased down by a dude who plays guitar.

F. Owner of a small bookstore downtown, loving and caring for troubled inner city kids, teaching them how to read.

TALLY UP YOUR SCORE

If you got mostly A's...
The glass slipper fits! You were made for **Prince Charming!**
The idea of the perfect happily ever after has always captivated you. You love guys who have it all together, the looks, the brains, and the heart...you want the whole package! You won't settle for anything less then what a princess deserves...which is a true prince. That's awesome girl! Let your heart keep dreaming as you continue waiting and praying for your prince charming. He will be more amazing then you dreamed possible!

If you got mostly B's...
Here he comes, riding in on his trusty steed! Girl, get ready for **Prince Phillip!** You dream of a guy who is adventurous, can make you laugh, and live life with passion and courage. You've been waiting for a guy like Phillip to gallop onto this page and escort you into the next chapter of life. Keep dreaming girl, and remember that God is writing your love story. He has written your Once-Upon-a-Time, and He will be faithful to complete your Happily-Ever-After!

If you got mostly C's...
Sha, la, la, la, kiss the girl! **Prince Eric** is your dream Disney dude! Your heart has longed for someone compassionate, caring, sensitive, and fearless...you truly desire a prince that looks like Jesus! Your Prince Eric is totally out there, and you can start praying for him today. Read on to find a special prayer to lift up over your prince!

If you got mostly D's...
You want a guy who's going to take you to a whole new world. Your ideal man looks like **Aladdin**. Opposites always attract, and it sounds like you desire someone who is going to show you life from a different perspective, sweetly steal your heart, and take you on a magic carpet ride!

If you got mostly E's...
Look out ladies! This girl is waiting for her **Flynn Rider!**

Okay, just admit it. That cocky, carefree, live-life on the edge attitude is pretty attractive to you. You may not be the type of girl who likes to take risks, so you feel the need to find someone who will bring out the "crazy" side of your personality. The Flynn Riders in this world are special. They've got so much potential inside to become strong, caring, world-changing guys...but as we know, guys like this can also use a little extra prayer! Read on to discover a really cool prayer you can speak over your future Flynn Rider!

If you got mostly F's...
You're a beauty who could easily fall in love with a beast like **Prince Adam!** You have eyes to see unlocked potential in the guys around you. Not every girl has the special ability to look at the Beast and see something beyond that...but you see with the eyes of a princess, and proclaim that he is a prince! You're probably looking forward to the day that you can dance around to a tale as old as time, song as old as rhyme...and see your love story reach it's Happily-Ever-After. Hang in there girl! The Author is creating something beautiful.

~*~

I believe that God has chosen a Prince Charming for me. I believe he has one for you as well! He's out there somewhere and is growing in his faith and character just like you are! Here's an example of Disney Prince Prayers you can pray over your future man!

Lord I pray that my Prince Phillip...
would know that I'm his princess worth fighting for. Make him gutsy and determined to serve you with his whole heart. Make him bold like Paul and gentle like David. I pray that he would be in it for the long haul, and that he would look like You. May he spell out the true definition of love. Make him to be patient and kind, keeping no record of wrongs. May he truly be a man operating at his highest God-given potential.

Lord I pray that my Prince Adam...
would be humble. Guard him from pride. Protect him from selfishness. Help me to be selfless in our relationship and, like Princess Belle, to have patient tenderness to call out and encourage the Prince I see in him. Wash his heart and mind with the water of Your Word so that our relationship can be clean, pure, and lovely before You.

Lord I pray that my Aladdin...
would be guarded from deception. Protect him from the lying, manipulating enemy. Make my man true, real, and genuine. Remind him that he doesn't have to be perfect...just real. May he never pretend to be something he's not and help our relationship be transparent. Help us to encourage each other and share not only good times, but also fears, tears, and forgiveness.

Lord I pray that my Flynn Ryder...
would be charming, witty, and attractive! Make his God given personality shine. Guard him from getting puffed up, being afraid of what others think, and putting on a mask of bravado. Help me to always encourage, uplift, and think about him positively. I desire to be his biggest admirer, cheerleader, and fan girl! Protect him from other girls who might try to snatch him up. Make him all mine!

Lord I pray that my Prince Charming...
would look like You! I ask that He would know where true perfection comes from...You and You alone. Mold His heart to be like Yours. Remind him that he is predestined to be conformed to the image of Christ. Lead him by Your Spirit and encourage Your amazing son!

Lord I pray that my Prince Eric...
would battle fiercely against the enemy's wicked schemes. Make him a warrior who will take your kingdom by force! Teach him how to use the Sword of your Word to fight for righteousness, justice, and those who cannot speak up for themselves. I pray that he would have a strong desire to protect and guard me!

Lord I pray that my Peter Pan...
would have a childlike faith. Nurture and encourage those childhood dreams, those desires You've placed deep inside him. Give him the faith to move mountains and reach every dream You've placed inside him. Remind him that with You all things are possible. Restore a childlike wonder as he enters Your kingdom and learns to fly with You. Faith, trust, and pixie dust.

Lord I pray that my Prince Naveen...
would be mature in You. Remove all the immature, frog-like behavior. Make him a leader. Fix his heart on You and on being devoted to his

future wife. Help him to avoid the temptation of other girls, of alcohol, drugs, and all sorts of worldly things that would try to get him off track. They will not prevail, but instead the promises over his life will conquer. He is your son and my prince! Help me not to be falling for frogs along the way, but to keep all my love stored up for him.

Lord I pray that my Captain John Smith...
would have perseverance. Enable him with Your grace to push through trials, live above the influence of this world, and fight for what he believes in. Make him a pioneer of change who will cut down trees and hills of impossibility and be a forerunner to pave the way for other guys! Make him a bold and courageous leader like Joshua, ready his hands and fingers for war on behalf of this generation, and make me like his Pocahontas who can partner with, serve, protect and love him.

Lord I pray that my Prince...
would be brave, willing to change and be molded into who he was created to be, relentless in his pursuits, and handsome in heart, yet with his own set of flaws. May he be courageous, still possessing a healthy amount of childlike wonder and faith, eager to forgive, and never stop fighting for me. If I'm expecting a prince, I must be transformed into a princess. Help me to grow in honor, character and royalty. Thank You for my dear prince. I know he's on the way.

~*~

When Life Feels Like A Taylor Swift Song

You totally weren't expecting this. It's a typical Monday morning. You stumble into class, half asleep, wishing you hadn't stayed up so late to finish watching *Pride and Prejudice*. All that's on your mind is what you'll be having for lunch. You wonder if the greasy cafeteria pizza will miraculously taste better this afternoon. Without warning, he walks through the door.

You're breathless. If you didn't know any better, you'd have sworn Taylor Swift's hit song, "Love Story," was playing in the background. You blink. He's not wearing the vintage Prince Charming outfit.

But he might as well be.

He sits down at the desk beside you and asks to borrow a pencil. Your mouth goes dry. You open it up, but no words come out. A friendly smile slips across his face as he shakes his shaggy blonde hair. He turns to ask the girl beside him for a pencil. Yeah, sure. Her mouth works fine.

The rest of the class you can't focus on math. All those numbers blur and dance across your page because the new boy is sitting right next to you! You find yourself doodling hearts in the margins of your notebook. Your Algebra homework has turned into a hodgepodge of whimsical doodles that spell his name. You walk home feeling like you're on Cloud Nine and your friends ask what's wrong with you. Where is your mind? What can you say?

You get home, float up the stairs, close the door behind you, and sink onto your bed. You hug your pillow, close your eyes and squeal. It's love! If the scene above describes how you feel every time a cute guy enters the scene, you're not the only one. He might be the new kid in town, a movie star, or your best guy friend that you've known since kindergarten but all of a sudden started to notice him in a new way. You don't know how it happened or why...but suddenly your heart feels like it's tumbling around in the washing machine. With all these emotional butterflies and feelings whirling around inside, what's a girl to do?

With so many attractive Prince Charming wannabes out there, it's easy for a girl to fall in and out of love every few months! As we grow older, we begin to notice that our lives feel more and more like a Taylor Swift song.

Has anyone ever put these three words together in a sentence? Boy + crazy + your name?

Maybe you feel like you have a tendency to fall head over heels in love with every boy who has one of the following characteristics:

A. A head of hair like Justin Bieber.

B. A silky singing voice that sounds like milk chocolate.

C. A killer "smolder" like Flynn Rider.

Most of us have fallen into a serious infatuation with "Mr. Adorable" somewhere along the way.

I'm about to share a story with you, torn straight from the worn-out pages of my journal. So please, proceed at your own risk...

My "Mr. Adorable" obsession was with a teen rock-star who probably needed a haircut. Nick Jonas sang his way into my heart on a toasty afternoon in August when I was fourteen- years-old. He appeared on Channel Mickey Mouse, prancing around like a little kid on the playground with his brothers, crooning something about being the "Kids of the Future."

My admiration of the youngest curly head in the Jonas trio grew, slowly tumbling around in my heart until it sprouted into something that felt like love. We're talking Starbursts, Skittles, and fireworks here! My friend bought their album and let me borrow it, and the headphones got me hooked.

How could I be so infatuated with someone I'd never met?

He was a superstar that lived a trillion miles away. I never went to any of their concerts or plastered my walls with posters, but Mr. Adorable consumed so much of my thought life, I probably could've shown a photograph to my Grandma and told her Nick was my boyfriend!

You see, it wasn't so much his voice, personality or the hair. It was more the idea of him. The perfection. The charismatic, adorable, sweet, sensitive guy that Disney marketed to me as the perfect boyfriend.

The image of my dream boy had become exactly that; a dream. The sad, pathetic part was that Nick Jonas didn't know I existed. He probably never would either.

It took a while for me to realize, that as I inflated the image of this guy in my mind, he began filling up a lonely, aching place in my heart. Nick was filling up the God-gap, the place in my heart that was supposed to be solely for God. I had crowned a new king in my heart.

I didn't realize the truth of my condition until the Holy Spirit whispered to the quiet places of my soul, "Whatever sits on the throne of your heart, is your god." Talk about conviction! Was God really telling me that I had crowned this flesh and blood human being as a lowercase god?

Mmm...hmm. Sometimes a girl has to be hit with a two-by-four to wake up and pay attention. The words were whispered ever so softly, but they might as well have been spoken by Ty Pennington with a megaphone! Let's just say, I mentally broke up with my imaginary beau before God had the chance to whisper the next sentence to me.

He continued to tell me that it *breaks His heart* when girls look to guys - mere human beings - for attention, affection, and adoration. He knows that we long for someone to ride in and rescue us, but Christ already has. "Oh my goodness," I hear you say, "are you actually suggesting that we girls place guys so high upon pedestals that we put them in the place of God!? You have got to be kidding me! No one does that!"

Uhhh...ever been to a popular boy band concert?

Throngs of weeping, screaming, hysterical girls display their love for the newest teen heart throb at these shows. Fan girls are amazing. They love extravagantly. They worship freely. Psh, they don't care what anyone else thinks! They are faithful and devoted. They buy every C.D. and memorize every lyric.

"Hold up!" I hear you bouncing out of your chair again, "Just because I like a guy doesn't mean I want to scream and throw roses at him! I'm not insane like those girls. You can't possibly compare a real life crush with what those girls are doing."

I hear you Sister. Some of us would *never* act that crazy for a guy. Those fans are displaying affection for who they love. And we all do that in a different way. Maybe you don't compete for your crush's attention, maybe you've never even talked to him. But are you thinking about him constantly?

Our minds think about what we love, adore and what is important to us. As girls, we were made to worship. The desire to love and passionately give up our lives for something bigger than ourselves is totally natural. God placed that in us. Only, when we choose to spend all our God-given passion on a guy, it's like we're worshiping the created being, rather than the Creator. (Check out Romans 1:25.)

"So what are you saying?" you frown as you cross your arms, getting ready to toss this book out the window. "Are you saying that girls aren't supposed to like guys? That having crushes is wrong? We are female! What do you expect us to be, holy nuns?!

In a word? No. If you think about it, obsession is a good thing. Falling in love and having that passionate drive is totally natural. God gave us a one-track mind so that we can set our heart on something and then chase after it.

So why are we spending this amazing, God-given capacity to love and worship with everything we are, on guys?

Because we desire perfection. We all wish to find that perfect someone we can spend the rest of our lives adoring. But that guy you're spending all your time day-dreaming about isn't really perfect. He has flaws. Major ones. Ones that you would probably run away and hide from if you knew about. This guy cannot love you the way that you want to be loved, perfectly and completely. Yes, he could try, and he might even do an amazing job at it. But not even the best boyfriend can compare to the kind of soul-hugging love that God is offering. No boy can rescue you from what you cannot see; those things warring against your soul. (Check out Ephesians 6:12.) I get it. You're growing concerned, wondering...is she anti-boy?

No, I am not, and neither is God! He desires you to someday be radically loved by a spectacular young man who cherishes you as much as Christ does. God isn't anti-love story. He is the author of every good and perfect fairytale.

Truth is, it's gotta feel mighty feel good to have a pair of arms to fall into, a guy to protect us when we go to the grocery store, or someone to write cute messages on our Facebook walls. But at the end of the day, no guy knows how to make you feel perfectly loved. He doesn't know how to give you just what you need. Sure, he can learn. And if he's the right guy, then he will learn. With God's help, he can become really fantastic at loving you!

But how can he know you inside out and tend to your *every* need? This guy didn't make you. He doesn't know every thought and every word before it comes out of your mouth. He doesn't know how many hairs are on your head. And he didn't save you.

Psalm 146:3 says, "Do not put your trust in princes, in mortal men who cannot save." (FYI, that was written by a King! Even he knew that he could only do so much!)

We try to decorate human guys as princes and kings. We place on them such great expectations. But it is not fair to ask them to rescue us when Someone already has.

The reason we wish the men around us were perfect is because we 池e missing the One who is! Jesus is honestly so ridiculously amazing that if we could truly see His beauty, no human guy this side of eternity could ever measure up.

Try to think about it like this: You're a princess who is magnificently loved by the Prince of Heaven. He is crazy about you and wants all your attention. He wants your secrets, your fears, your love, and your thoughts. He wants you to be *obsessed* with Him because that's the way He feels about you.

Don't you think it hurts your Prince's heart when you toss flirty pebbles of affection at the back windows of the guys in your neighborhood? Your Prince wants all of you. The very best of you. Not just your leftover love.

Someday, He would be thrilled to give you a human dude who can help reflect a little of His love and take care of you. But even when you're loved by the most amazing man ever, it will still seem so microscopic compared to Christ's love for you! If you're anything like me, you might be noticing a problem. You know where your mind is supposed to be fixed, on the Prince of Heaven, yet you can't stop thinking about all the earthly princes roaming around!

You, like I did, see what you're supposed to do. I knew what the goal was, but I felt lost, way out in left field somewhere. I just couldn't stop thinking about him! It didn't matter how much I rationalized it:

"Livy, he's a superstar, he'll never know you're alive, doesn't know your last name..." That didn't help. I was still thinking about him. What could I do? I could only find one answer.

Talk to my Creator. I mean, God should be responsible for how I feel. He's the one that made boys so stinkin' cute! While crushing, it's easy to feel like we want to talk to everyone (and I mean everyone!) about it (your BFF, your Mom, your dog, your FB...) except God.

Why do we keep these things from Him? Maybe it's because we think it's too silly, or serious, for Him to be concerned.

But the truth is, He loves when we talk with Him about boys. I have discovered that the Holy Spirit hosts the best sleepover parties ever.

Once I started whispering to the Lord in the middle of the night about how adorable I thought Nick Jonas was, God started to steer the direction of our conversation.

I started thinking about how unfair it was that God made someone so perfect and that I couldn't have him. I was angry. So I told God. I asked

Him what the heck He was thinking! I told Him how I saw things. I asked who I was supposed to end up with. "What, am I supposed to be lonely and single forever?"

That's when the conversation took a dramatic turn. I felt the Holy Spirit's sweet presence blow across my heart, "What I've got planned for you is better than Nick Jonas."

Major jaw dropper! Ever since that moment, I've been on this crazy, outta control roller coaster ride, as God has helped me navigate through the wild world of boys, and began revealing to me who my true Prince Charming is. Sounds exciting, doesn't it?
You don't have to be reading about it. You can be living it!

Start a midnight conversation with Christ about your crush. And watch as He takes you on a crazy adventure to the throne room of His heart.

Remember, God wants to hear from you, even more than you want to talk to Him! He will always be listening, and nothing is ever too silly or serious to talk about with Him. The reality of this moment is that you will feel this way about another guy somewhere, someday. Even though right now he feels like everything, *don't* make him your world.

It's easy to inflate a mere human being, to elevate him to the level of a god. It's easy to think of him as your hero and see him as everything you've ever dreamed. But he's not perfect. If you place such high expectations upon a human boy, it'll be all too easy to wind up with a broken heart and teardrops on your guitar. I've been there.

It can be a tough truth to swallow, but not all guys are *men*. They're still growing up. They act immature. They do stupid things. They don't always treat girls like the princesses that we are. If you really want to end up with a true prince charming, you might be waiting awhile. Most boys are frogs in the local frog pond who have yet to turn into royal princes.

So how can you keep yourself from becoming totally enthralled with him while he's still a frog?

"Above everything else guard your heart, because from it flow the springs of life..." {Proverbs 4:23}

This ancient Biblical Proverb advises us to guard our hearts, because everything we do flows from there. Full, healthy hearts love life and appreciate beauty. Broken, bitter hearts feel depressed and discouraged, and hurt others because they have been hurt. But how can a princess keep her heart safe when an adorable prince is tossing pebbles at her window?

"Do not be anxious about anything, but in every situation, by prayer and petition, with thanksgiving, present your requests to God. And the peace of God, which transcends all understanding, will guard your hearts and minds in Christ Jesus." {Philippians 4:6-7}

The scripture above tells us to cast our cares on God, and His *peace* will guard our hearts! We don't have to be our own armor bearers. We don't have to stay away from boys, stand on the other side of the room and dare not touch them with a ten-foot pole! We can learn to relate with our guy friends, encourage them, and learn to be a safe friend. We can practice being princesses while we wait for them to become princes.

This verse tells us that our hearts will be kept safe and guarded, just as long as we cast our cares on God. What does this mean? It means if we talk to God, stay in constant communication with Him, and abide in His love; *HE* will protect us and our emotions.

All you have to do is talk to Him! Let Him know how you feel about this guy. It's great to pray something like, "Lord, you've placed this guy in my life for a reason. Is it just to be friends and learn how to relate with guys, or will this someday turn into something more? Help me to be like Sleeping Beauty and don't let my heart wake up until it's time for love! Prepare me to be an amazing princess for my future prince."

"Finally brothers and sisters, whatever is true, whatever is noble, whatever is right, whatever is lovely, whatever is admirable - if anything is excellent or praiseworthy - think about such things."
{Philippians 4:8}

Grab your journal and make a list of all the things you like about him. What are the qualities you find so attractive in him? Is it physical features, personality, or common interests? Write down his positive qualities. If it's noble, admirable, or praiseworthy, write it down! This will help you realize why you like him. Is it just his cute looks, or is it his funny personality? Is it because he's kind to everyone or because he's showing you a lil' bit of extra attention?

Make your list and then give it to God! Let the Lord know all the reasons you like him and then surrender. Ask Him to help you keep your heart safe.

Now, make a second list. Create a list of things that you are thankful for, your goals, your dreams, and aspirations. Write down what's important to you in life. What would you like to accomplish? Would you like to be married someday? Write that down. Would you like to travel? Jot it! Make this list totally you, and remember that your goals reach further than just finding the right guy.

Tuck these lists into a safe place. They will remind you of who you are, what you're looking for and what's important to you. It will help you to keep focused on what really matters and to live with extravagant purpose!

~*~

No Frogs Allowed

Are you kissing frogs? I've been there, done that. Unfortunately, I wasn't raised in a devout Christian home. I knew a tad about Jesus but I didn't know Him intimately, so I was boy crazy, really boy crazy. In Fifth Grade alone I had *sixteen* boyfriends (yes, I used to keep count).

I always wanted to find my prince and started my hunt for him as early as Kindergarten. Guess what I discovered? They were all frogs. Not one of them was a true prince, a hero; someone I could trust my heart with, who would protect it and care tenderly for it. I couldn't understand why none of these boys could love me the way I believed I loved them. (Looking back, I realize what I felt for my fifty-three exes was *not* true love. It was actually worldly infatuation, based only on physical attraction...aka lust. It was emotional satisfaction because I liked the attention I was receiving. I call guys who don't know and love Jesus, "frogs." Sure, they have potential to become a prince if they give their lives to Jesus, but until then, they are to be avoided at all costs.

In my eBook, *Kiss A Frog, Miss the Prince*, I focus on four frogs we girls can jump into a swamp with.

1. The Infatuated Frog
This is a guy who can't get enough of you; in the beginning. He texts you all the time, he skips school to see you, and he spends money he doesn't really have on you. You're the little fly he cannot get his big, froggy eyes off of. It doesn't take long for him to tell you he loves you. Here's what he doesn't realize: He isn't in love with you, he's infatuated with you.

Infatuation is defined as a "foolish, all-absorbing, short-lived passion." In other words, infatuation fades and then eventually dies. Then he moves on to another girl and repeats the same cycle of infatuation.

The Bible says real love never fails. It isn't self-seeking either. The infatuated frog is with you for how you make him feel, not because he wants to honor and serve you as Christ calls him to. So, if you don't want to end up being dumped, I highly suggest hopping over this frog.

2. The Rebel Frog
Have you ever dated a bad-boy? I have, too many times. These frogs tend

to be on the rougher side. They're considered cool because of their "I don't care what anyone thinks" attitude. They also have serious issues: a severely dysfunctional family, anger problems, a drug addiction, anything very problematic that will eventually taint your relationship.

Many of us girls get entangled with these kind of guys because of our nurturing nature. We greatly desire to "help them." At least that was the case for me. However, since these guys are not yet healed by Jesus, they are walking around with a double-edged sword sticking out of their hearts. You will eventually get sliced by their pain! Since his heart is so broken and messed up, he cannot possibly love and treat you in a healthy way. Don't waste your time trying to heal him with your love; only Jesus can do that in a person's life. You'll just end up breaking your own precious heart.

3. The Controlling Frog
This frog's dangerous. Well, all frogs are dangerous, but this one especially. He has control issues because deep down he's insecure. He feels a sick sense of power if he can get you to bend to his will. And if you give him your body, he becomes really controlling because now he thinks you're some object that belongs to him, rather than the precious daughter of God he is entrusted with to protect and care for. If you don't want to become emotionally or physically abused, RUN from this frog ASAP!

4. The Deceitful Frog
This frog knows how to lie! He's a great actor. If you're not careful, he can even trick you into thinking he's a Christian. He's a frog in prince's clothing and can use his words to deceive you. Don't be fooled by his sweet talk but study his "fruit." Is he tempting you to do impure things with him? Does he try to justify sinning? Make sure you never ignore red flags; and that goes for any guy. If you're a Christian, the Holy Spirit will warn you about a boy who's trying to pursue you, yet isn't a prince of God's kingdom. No matter how cute the frog, do not ignore those signs, or you will get slimed. Worst of all, you may end up marrying a frog and never return to Jesus again.

So who should I be looking for?

The Rescued Frog

Here's a guy who lets Jesus save him and thus he is transformed from a frog into a prince. He isn't perfect like the King, but since he follows Jesus he will love you better than any frog ever can. Not only will he love you like the princess you are, but he will cause you to grow closer to Jesus, not drag you farther away from Him like frogs do. That's the kind of man you want as a husband; one who is a genuine Christian, who has died to his old, froggy ways and is now a prince in God's Kingdom. He truly desires to live for God. How you can tell a true prince from a frog? By his fruit. Does he obey Jesus and walk like Him? Is he patient, kind, gentle, self-controlled, loving and peaceful? Does he want to wait for you until marriage because he knows to do otherwise is sin?

A prince will protect your heart, not break it. He will respect you, not take advantage of you.

~*~

About the Author:

Natasha Sapienza is a daughter of the King, a wife, and mother. She has written two e-books and is currently writing a YA fantasy trilogy. To learn more about waiting for your prince and being content in your relationship with Jesus, visit her blog: www.betterthanprincecharming.com

Dating, Waiting, and Just Totally Relating

1. Still Single? Learn to Enjoy the Journey

This may be the only time in your life that you'll be single, so do it well. How well you live today will open blessings for your future. There's no need to be obsessed about finding someone to marry. Think of *Ella Enchanted*. She was so focused on her task of finding her fairy godmother, to undo the curse that was upon her life, that chasing after Prince Char was the last thing on her mind. She was not like her twin stepsisters, Hattie and Olive, who were infatuated with him, chasing him when they saw him and trying every scheme possible to get to be his princess. Needless to say, Prince Char literally had to run away and hide from them! Of course, it was Ella the prince chose to marry. Being desperate for a boyfriend isn't attractive to most boys.

For a Biblical example, let's look at Ruth. When Ruth's husband died, she became determined and focused on what God wanted her to do. She was busy looking after her mother-in-law, working hard, and gleaning in the field. She made God her priority and trusted Him to provide, despite her negative circumstances.

"So Ruth, the Moabitess, said to Naomi, 'Please let me go to the field, and glean heads of grain after him in whose sight I may find favour.'" {Ruth 2:2}

Ruth was not desperately looking around for her next husband to come along. Just like Ella in the movie, this made her stand out to Boaz, the most eligible bachelor whom she later married.

2. Prince Charming is Not Your Answer

If you're lonely as a single girl, then you'll likely be lonely in a marriage. Are you insecure? Then you'll be insecure in marriage. Allow God to transform you through his Word, the renewal of your mind and the Holy Spirit. Ask God to show you areas of your life you may need to improve on before your prince arrives.

Most of all, focus on the love that God has for you, "(so) that Christ may dwell in your hearts through faith; that you, being rooted and grounded in love, may be able to comprehend with all the saints what is the width and length and depth and height - to know the love of Christ which

passes knowledge; that you may be filled with all the fullness of God."
{Eph. 3:17-19}

The more you know and believe His love, the more you'll be empowered to love others. You need to be secure in your relationship with Him first of all. The Lord Jesus will always be your husband, so cultivate His presence, spend time with Him, talk to Him, listen to Him, and develop your relationship with Him. You have the precious gift of time that will disappear once you're married. Spend your time wisely. Sitting at His feet is the most constructive use of your time, for now and for the future.

"A wife of noble character who can find? She is worth far more than rubies." {Proverbs 31:10}

It is to our credit, therefore, to be virtuous or noble; to put the needs of others before ourselves; to be loving, kind and gracious; to be generous to those in need; and to worship the Lord. These are all things we can put into practice regardless of our marital status.

Ask God to highlight any areas of your life where you need to develop or improve. Do you have any bad habits? Is there any part of your emotional health that needs his healing touch? If you feel insecure now, you'll be insecure in your marriage. If you fly off the handle when you're single, you'll be just the same after the wedding.

3. Do Something With Your Life!
Think of all those things you would love to do in life. What dreams do you have in your heart? Maybe you're interested in doing charity work at home or abroad? You could spend time traveling, write a book, learn photography, start a business or write a blog. You may not have the chance when you're married. Remember, you're blessed to be a blessing; so use your blessing of time to benefit others as well.

God wants us to be in relationship with others too. How's your relationship with your parents? Your friends? What about other women in the Church or colleagues at work? You need these people and they need you. God put them in your life for a reason. Use this season to develop your relationships with them. Be the best friend you can be. Be the best daughter you can be. Compliment them, encourage them, treat them, make an effort to call them and think of activities to do with them. Go shopping, go out for lunch, watch movies together. When you're married, you won't have as much time to spend with them, but you are still going to need them. Invest time with them now (and I don't just mean communicate with them on Facebook!)

As a child of God, we're each designed for great things in all areas, not just marriage and motherhood. Most romantic comedies, soaps, dramas, or even the other girls at school try to entice you into believing the way of the world is better, that having multiple partners throughout your life is healthy or even exciting. But you're better than this. You are the daughter of the Creator of the Universe; His most treasured possession. You're in a season of preparation for whatever He has for you. Make right choices and do your best in your season of singleness. You have such an exciting life ahead of you.

"Sing O barren woman, you who have not borne, break forth unto singing and cry aloud you who have not laboured with child! For more are the children of the desolate than the children of the married woman,' says the LORD." {Isaiah 54:1}

4. Proceed with Caution and Beware of the Charmers
"Many a man claims to have unfailing love, but a faithful man who can find?" {Proverbs 20:6}

Beware of the charmers, girls. I once knew a guy who was the friendliest man on the surface. He was chatty, funny, and seemingly considerate. He would wash my car, offer to drive me places and offer to cook for me. He also flattered me with compliments and said all those things that women want to hear. He was also a liar who thought it was OK to have multiple girlfriends. {Proverbs 6:17}

Then there are the ones that are the life and soul of the party. They're friendly and sociable and usually very popular. A good personality doesn't equal strong character. Just because someone has lots of friends and tells jokes, doesn't mean he can weather the storm. There are men who are like this but as soon as problems come about, they walk away from the marriage! Unfortunately, just because someone is a Christian doesn't mean he's a man of his word or knows how to respect and treat someone well.

5. Focus on the Greatest Love Story Relationship of All

Doesn't every girl want to be treated as though she is a princess? Is there someone out there who loves you and sees you as though you are the only girl alive, someone who tells you you're beautiful and the apple of his eye? Someone who wants the very best for you; who will fight for you, protect you, comfort you and provide for you; someone who always listens to you and won't ever let you down; someone who loves you so much he would die for you? Sadly for most girls, they seek this person in all the wrong places and end up unhappy, disappointed and unfulfilled. Sleeping Beauty was rescued by a brave, strong and mighty prince who fought and never gave up. What princess wouldn't want a relationship with him?

When we become born again, we begin the most exciting relationship we'll ever know or experience! Up until this point, we may have known about God; we may have heard others talk about Him, we may have read the Bible or heard it preached in Church. But it takes the Holy Spirit to reveal both God's true nature and His love for us. Then we walk with Him, talk with Him, and hear His voice and truly fellowship with Him.

"It is for freedom that Christ has set us free. Stand firm, then, and do not let yourselves be burdened again by a yoke of slavery." {Gal 5:3}

God does not want us to be confined to rules; He wants our hearts.

"For sin shall not have dominion over you: for ye are not under the law, but under grace." {Rom 6:14}

We don't need to earn blessings from God any longer, as we are made continually righteous through Jesus. We are highly-favoured children.

"And if by grace, then is it no more of works: otherwise grace is no more grace. But if it be of works, then it is no more grace: otherwise work is no more work." {Rom 11:6}

We are free to be the princesses we were born to be! Imagine how Sleeping Beauty felt to be suddenly awakened from a 100-year sleep? Consider the freedom! His heart toward us will never alter regardless of our performance. It is an 'Abba' Father relationship.

"For ye have not received the spirit of bondage again to fear; but ye have received the Spirit of adoption, whereby we cry, Abba, Father." {Rom. 8:15}

"...accepted in the Beloved," {Eph. 1:6} through what Christ has done.

He "is a friend that sticks closer than a brother." {Prov. 18:24}

He wants us blessed and loved and well taken care of. "Fear not, little flock; for it is your Father's good pleasure to give you the kingdom" {Luke 12:32], for this is His nature. Those who accept Him enter His Kingdom.

When God's love is established in our hearts, we are empowered to love Him in return and love others as a result; making this the most important relationship we can have. We develop a natural desire to spend time with Him, to seek and worship Him. We want to get to know Him better, listen to Him and do His will. Living holy becomes a fruit of the relationship, not a requirement. Our relationship with God isn't based on our goodness any more, but on Christ's goodness.

When we're in a relationship with God, the Word by means of the Holy Spirit enables us to see situations from a spiritual perspective. There's an assurance, a peace in our hearts that "in all situations God works for the good." We don't need to panic in a crisis because we have a helper in the Holy Spirit and knowledge that "nothing is impossible" for Him. We have an "elpis" hope, the "confident and joyful expectation of good" that the world doesn't have. We don't need to depend upon natural resources. Isn't that incredible? That even in the midst of trouble, we still feel priceless and special; worth more than the jewels of any earthly kingdom.

Abraham was able to see with his spiritual eyes. "Lift your eyes now and look from the place where you are: northward, southward, eastward, and westward." {Gen 13:14} When we read the scriptures, we're given wisdom that helps us make right choices. We hear God's voice, and have increased spiritual memory so we're able to recall crucial verses in time of need. It says Abraham,"who, contrary to hope, in hope believed, so that he became the father of many nations, according to what was spoken, 'So shall your descendants be.' And not being weak in faith, he did not consider his own body, already dead (since he was about a hundred years old), and the deadness of Sarah's womb. He did not waver at the promise of God through unbelief, but was strengthened in faith, giving glory to God, and being fully convinced that what He had promised He was also able to perform." {Rom 4:18-21}

It is possible to be in the middle of the fiercest storm but be "walking on cloud nine!" The Bible teaches us that the seed of the Word has to be planted in our hearts. Nothing works outside of the Word. A relationship with God without the Scriptures is difficult, as our hearts would just become too hardened and our faith would fail. We would lose that sense of God's love and begin to strive unnecessarily. Our minds would start to go in the opposite direction; we'd lose sense of the hope we once knew as the doubts and fears begin to overpower us. We'd feel distant as our faith is replaced by the cares and concerns of the world.

This is the opposite of resisting the devil and actually empowers him to keep us bound. The Bible is our "daily bread," to nourish, strengthen, protect and transform us into "the likeness of Jesus." It is God's provision. It is everything we need to live that "princess life."

"And be not conformed to this world: but be ye transformed by the renewing of your mind, that ye may prove what is that good, and acceptable, and perfect, will of God." {Rom 12:2}

As children of God, we partner with Him. We progress as we relationship with Him into strong women (or men) of God who show a likeness to Him. We sow seeds into people's hearts and pray for those seeds to grow. We allow God to pour out His love into us so it's overflowing into those around us. We use the gifts He's given us to give Him glory so the world can see that He is good. 'He that spared not his own Son, but delivered him up for us all, how shall he not with him also freely give us all things?" {Rom 8:32}

No one will ever love us as much as our perfect Heavenly Father. Praise God that we have the awesome privilege to be His children and His bride!

~*~

About the Author:
Lorna Penn graduated with BA honors in German from the University of Manchester in the UK. Then she became a primary school teacher, specializing in preschool education.

She is actively part of the chaplaincy team which ministers the love of God to patients at her local hospital, and she loves to support and mentor baby Christians at her church who are new in the faith.

Let's Get Real: Modest Fashion

An Oxymoron?

Perhaps you've heard the words "modest" and "fashion" paired together. Take a deep breath, and trust me on this one. "Modest Fashion" isn't an oxymoron. Those two words can be paired together without getting in a huge fight with one another.

When we hear the word "modesty" we instantly think of floor length jean skirts! We remember the Amish family we saw skipping into Burger King wearing bonnets on top of their heads. Modesty can place some frightening images of fashion crimes in our minds!

Many of us have grown up in Christian families and church communities, and we hear the word "modesty" so much that it's easy to roll our eyes and zone out. Who wants to hear another sermon about righteousness, legalism and modesty? Not me!

Girls, what we're about to discuss may be like nothing you've ever heard in a sermon before. We're about to dish on the real "why" behind being modest. Fasten your seat belt as we get ready to embark into the mind of guys! That's right, we're going to explore how they think about girls, sex, and modesty. Uh oh, this could get really interesting...

Guys Are Visual. What Does That Mean For Us?

Excuse my lack of "Christian manners" when I say this, but we are living in a sex-saturated culture. You know what I'm talking about. It doesn't take much looking around to realize that we're being marketed all sorts of sexy thoughts – heated movie scenes, song lyrics, and sultry magazine covers. It's all around us. In fact, we've grown quite accustomed to it, and it all feels pretty normal!

As females, some of us haven't given much thought to our culture's obsession with sex. But this has been on the boys' brains for a while now. Young men are given many opportunities throughout the day to fill their thoughts with details of the female body. They see tempting images on television, the internet, and even in our school hallways.

You've probably heard a pastor or friend say, "Don't cause a brother in Christ to be tempted!" Why would they say that, and what does that mean exactly?

The truth is that guys are visual. They are wired differently than we are, and male eyes help drive their imaginations. While it can sound disgustingly repulsive to us girls, many guys have sexual fantasies with girls they see throughout the day, in the playground of their minds. These constant temptations can give way to something called lust.

Lust. Eww! It's an idea that not many girls are acquainted with. For example, when many of us like a guy, we think "Oh, he's so darling, look how cute he is when he holds a puppy dog, I hope we can go to Disney World together, I love his hair..."

For guys, it's a little different. When they see an attractive girl, they sometimes struggle to keep their thoughts out of the bedroom. Jesus (who knows the mind of every person) understands the struggle that guys have to keep their thoughts nice and clean. He told a group of His young followers,"You have heard that it was said, 'You shall not commit adultery.' But I tell you that anyone who looks at a woman lustfully has already committed adultery with her in his heart."

Jesus understood the thoughts that randomly pop up in a guy's mind. He wanted His best friends to see that lusting after someone is the same as having sex with them outside of marriage. Totally against God's commandment of purity! This helped Jesus' followers see the difference between love and lust. I think it's crazy that Jesus addressed this problem back in the day when all the local girls were wearing robes. If guys were struggling with women wearing drab outfits who showed no skin whatsoever, imagine how much more difficult it must be today! Every day of their lives, our male friends' minds are constantly being bombarded with tempting thoughts and images of the female body. Of course, it is their choice what they wish to do with these thoughts. Just because a filthy thought pops into his head, doesn't make him guilty. It's his choice whether to dismiss the thought and think about something else or continue to dwell on the image.

When I first learned that boys thought like this, I was quite disgusted. I crossed my arms and thought, "That's so gross! They need to grow up! I should be able to wear a mini-skirt without guys thinking nasty thoughts. I should be able to wear whatever I want, 'cause it's cute!"

I quickly learned that my definition of cute and a guy's idea of cute are actually quite different. After reading *For Young Women Only: What Every Girl Should Know About How Guys Think*, I was a little shocked. Truth is, many items in our closet, like spaghetti-strap tops, low T's, short shorts, and mini-skirts, are not the innocent "cute" we think they are. Ask your Mom or any other girl, and she'll say, "That's so adorable!" Ask a guy and he'll think, "That's so sexy." Showing off cleavage and legs around our male friends help drive their lustful desires. It intensifies and increases those thoughts that say, "Gah, I have to have her. Like, right now."

Attention Feels Good
"Okay," I hear you say, "I get what you're saying, except...I kind of like the extra attention I get from guys when I dress suggestively. I know they might not be thinking pure thoughts, but it just feels so good to be adored!" You're not the only chick who feels like that. If we're honest, we all love the attention.

But how can we be confident in our own skin and cover up without feeling like we have to dress in a revealing way to get extra stares? Well, first of all, we have to understand how the guys think about this. When they glance at a girl in a mini-skirt, flirting to compete for her attention, it is done in a lustful desire for her body. The kind of attention received from showing off your God-given, feminine mystique is not the kind of attention we think it is. In a girl's mind, we believe that male attention equals male adoration. We believe that if he's looking at us, it must mean that he loves us! This is where so many of us girls get it wrong. If his eyes are enjoying your body, it doesn't mean that he likes your heart, personality, or brain. Sometimes we have to snap out of our fairytale dreams and realize the not-so-pretty truth behind what's going on in his brain. Just because he looks at and desires your body doesn't guarantee that he loves you...it doesn't even mean that he likes you!

I can hear you laughing, "Oh yeah right! I've seen the way guys act around the pretty, sexy girl at our school. They trip over themselves. They try to make her laugh. They totally like her."

I know it's hard to believe, but like Jordan Taylor from Blimey Cow says, "Sometimes a guy wants to eat the chocolate bar without having to pay for it." In other words, a guy can really, really like the sparkly wrapper (the outer shell, or body of a girl) without giving a second thought of care to who she is on the inside. Some guys don't want to make the long term investment of digging into their pockets, and counting up the cost of that chocolate-bar girl. They don't want to ask themselves, "How much will it cost for me to have her? What is she worth? Can I afford to love her with my life? Is she worth my life, my whole heart, and a lifetime commitment of marriage?"

Some guys skip the expensive payment of marriage and take what they want from her body without legally "owning" it, or having a right to share in the gift of her sexuality. In a supermarket, this would be considered stealing! But in our world today, this is considered normal.

Sex has become so cheap and common, that many girls view their sexuality as a low-priced party favor to share with whoever is interested. If a guy is interested in our body, we somehow feel validated, loved, adored and cared for. And our culture tells us that as long as we slap the word LOVE on it that it's totally legal and right! But this is where so many girls misinterpret his desire for sex as a promise of him saying, "I'll love you forever and always." But that's not what he is saying at all!

If he has not "paid" for your body, soul, and your whole heart with a wedding ring, he has no reason to stay committed or even connected to you. Don't confuse sex with love, because in a guy's mind it is not the same thing.

Guys are funny like that – they don't mind playing around and enjoying themselves with various females who stimulate sexual desires...but at the end of the day, their hearts truly desire someone who is gonna be much harder to catch. They desire someone who will make them work for what they want. Most guys really do want to find and marry the diamond in the rough. Not to say they won't use and enjoy what is easy, but in the long run, they will strive for what is a challenge.

Man was made with a natural drive to conquer the bad guy and impress his dream girl. Most men would love to rescue the damsel in distress, sword fight for her, and do whatever he has to do to spend the rest of his life with that one, not-so-easy girl. (And if they don't feel like that, they are not the type of guy you want anyway!)

Personally, I would like to be viewed as a treasure. I would like to be viewed as an expensive diamond, not a cheap knock-off brand. If a young man pursues me, the price will be high. He must give all of his attention, a life-long commitment, and a wedding ring of promise. And until then, I won't be giving out any free favors from my body!

I don't want to be the girl who says "Look, this is me! This is what I have to offer! Please, please, please pick me!"

Instead, I want to be a princess locked up in Rapunzel's tower, where the guy has to be persistent and prove his character before I let my hair down and allow him to get to know me. I don't want to lower myself out of the tower...he must find a way to climb up it! I would like to be the challenge, the one that he must fight for and win!

Cheap And Easy Or A Garden Locked Up?
So many girls are afraid of being the last one picked. They want to be the guy's first priority, the one that he notices and falls head over heels in love with. Wear clothes that show off your body, and trust me, he will notice.

But what if you choose to dress modestly, cover up and stand on the sidelines? Does that mean you'll be the last one picked? Will tons of guys pass you by before the right one finally finds you? Well...in a word...yes. If you choose to dress modestly, some guys may view you as "Best Friend" material, rather than "Girlfriend" material. If you choose to save both your heart and your body for your future spouse, you will have many guys who pass you by without giving you a second thought. But is it worth it? Absolutely.

There's something extra special about waiting. Most of us hate waiting in line at the store or our favorite restaurant. We desire that everything be quick and easy. We want everything ASAP! Imagine this: What if we had Christmas every morning? How special would that be? We would grow so tired of the packages, cleaning up the mess, all our crazy relatives, and those darn Christmas cookies. Instead, we only get Christmas once a year, which makes it a special, magical time. We have to wait TWELVE

MONTHS for it, and by Christmas Eve we are stoked. We can't wait until morning!

Just imagine how special it will be to open up the Heaven-sent package of sex with your spouse after you have waited for so long. Won't it be worth it then, and so much sweeter?

The Song of Solomon says, "Daughters of Jerusalem, I charge you: Do not arouse or awaken love until it so desires." (8:4)

King Solomon found that his bride wouldn't be an easy catch. He told her: "You are a garden locked up, my sister, my bride; you are a spring enclosed, a sealed fountain." (4:12)

Do you wish to be a garden locked up and wait to unwrap a spectacular gift on your wedding night? Or would you rather get the greasy fast-food, quick and instantaneous, McDonalds' version of this love feast? Wait on the Lord to write your transcending love story. Trust me, any time spent waiting on the Lord is never wasted. He knows what He is doing! He is the Author of every good and perfect fairy tale!

This One Is For The Boys
Let's say, for example, you've decided to be pure and wait for your future spouse. You've always known this was expected of you; you wear the purity ring and everything. You're a good girl, not the type to go out and do anything crazy, and you know the condition of your heart...but does that mean you still have to dress modestly?

You could say, "The only reason I should care about modesty is because I'm sending out a message to boys, right? That's still not reason enough for me to change what I wear. I know I'm a good girl. I should be able to wear whatever I want! You can't take away my freedom!"

You're right. It's a free country. And God never once said in the Bible, "Though shalt not wear a bikini." It's not in the ten commandments. As girls, we should be free to wear whatever we want! And honestly, we can! God isn't going to judge us for wearing a mini-skirt...honestly girls, He could care less about skirts. Instead, He is more concerned with the heart behind the clothes.

Let's take a quick look at someone from the Bible. Paul wasn't an expert fashion designer, but he did know a thing or two about life. In this time period everyone was freaked out about eating food in idol temples. It was the issue of the day, and everyone had divided thoughts, just like we do on modesty. Some say, "Don't show skin! Don't show knees!" Others say, "You can show a little as long as it's not TOO much," and others firmly say, "I can wear whatever I want!"

Paul was hearing many arguments. After stating his advice (that we are free in Christ and seriously can eat or drink whatever we like as long as we're loving God and putting Him first) he added:

"Be careful, however, that the exercise of your rights does not become a stumbling block to the weak. For if someone with a weak conscience sees you, with all your knowledge, eating in an idol's temple, won't that person be emboldened to eat what is sacrificed to idols? So this weak brother or sister, for whom Christ died, is destroyed by your knowledge. When you sin against them in this way and wound their weak conscience, you sin against Christ. Therefore, if what I eat causes my brother or sister to fall into sin, I will never eat meat again, so that I will not cause them to fall." (1 Corinthians 8:9-13)

We could say the same thing about clothing, right? Let's read it again, instead with clothes in mind. "Be careful, however, that the exercise of your rights (to wear whatever you like) does not become a stumbling block to the weak. For if someone with a weak conscience sees you (guys who are struggling to think pure thoughts), with all your knowledge, eating in an idol's temple (dressing immodestly), won't that person be emboldened to eat what is sacrificed to idols? (Won't he be tempted to linger on the image of your body?) So this weak brother, for whom Christ died, is destroyed by your knowledge. When you sin against them in this way and wound their weak conscience, you sin against Christ. Therefore, if what I eat (wear) causes my brother to fall into sin, I will never eat meat (dress immodestly) again, so that I will not cause them to fall."

Dressing modestly is an act of love to the guys in our lives. It's a way of saying, "Hey, I know you're struggling with this, and even though I have the right to wear whatever I want, I'm not going to because I want to help you out."

Choosing to put a totally cute top that you're absolutely drooling over, back on the rack because it's gonna tempt your guy friends, is an act of love that will not go without a reward!

The Bible says that you will be rewarded for your secret acts of love toward another. And isn't this one of them? Switching out those tiny shorts that make you feel totally cute for something a little longer, so that your weak brother won't be tempted? That's an honorable thing that nobody else will see except Christ.

Going the extra mile in love, to find clothes that won't trip up his mind, can be difficult but not impossible. Dressing modestly doesn't mean you have to sacrifice style. You can still look cute and be attractive! Dressing modestly simply means you're going out of your way to cover up what might be tempting to your guy friends. Sound simple enough? It is!

And in case you've been struggling with the lie that tells you modest fashion is ugly and impossible...it's not! You don't have to revamp your entire wardrobe to dress modestly. In fact, you probably have many of the essential pieces already!

Are you ready to learn some trendy fashion secrets of how you can be adorable and modest? Read on!

~*~

5 Fabulous Shopping Tips

1) Add a Pair of Leggings to Your Shortest Dresses:
No need to despair. You don't need to sacrifice cuteness on your favorite dress. Lucky for us, layers are totally in. Every girl should have a pair of white leggings. It's a closet must! Leggings come in handy for dresses and skirts, and add insta-classy flair to any outfit!

2) Summer Shorts: How Short is Short?
The question of the ages. How short is too short for my shorts? Everyone seems to have a different idea of what is acceptable. The easiest way to answer this question? Ask your Dad or your older brother. If he understands you're striving for modesty and that you want him to answer you honestly, he will! If there isn't a man in your life you can ask about this, I always try to keep shorts longer than my fingertips when my arms are stretched out straight. Personally, I feel like less leg is better, and the area above my knee caps really doesn't need to be seen by anyone. This gives a girl lots of creative options. Board shorts are quite popular. It's also fun to take a pair of Capris or old jeans, roll them up and embroider the leg cuffs. This gives me the length I want...and the cuteness!

3) Tank Tops are a Girl's Best Friend:
Huge shopping tip: don't be afraid to splurge on tanks! You'll discover that in the modest shopping world, tank tops are a girl's best friend! Tanks offer coverage for when you want to wear your favorite plunging top, a cool option to wear beneath crop tops, and they also add length to tops which don't offer coverage when you lean over to pick up a pencil. A fantastic rule for modest shopping: layer, layer, layer!

4) Dryer Tops:
While shopping at my favorite stores, sometimes I feel like all the tops in the Junior's section have been shrunk in the dryer. Nobody wants a top that shows lots of skin, but what about snug tops that hug all the right places? Personally, I think clingy tops are comfortable and feel nice. They also make a girl feel thin and trim! But when your top clings to your bust...let's be honest, your shirt might as well be see through! For a guy, his imagination knows no bounds. Help him keep his thoughts pure by opting for the next size up. You don't need to wear baggy shirts. But if

you're in the dressing room and feel like your shirt is giving you a tight hug, opt to try on the next biggest size. If it looks way too big and unflattering, that's okay. Put both shirts back and keep looking for something modest! You will find it! You just have to search a little harder.

5) Strappy is Tacky:
Got bra straps showing, or anything that might be perceived as one? (Such as a thin tank top, cami, or spaghetti strap?) In my opinion, strappy is tacky. It hints at what's happening underneath your shirt, and you really don't want anyone's mind going there!

~*~

A New Kind of Model:
Interview with Rachel Lee Carter

Rachel Lee Carter was living the life that so many of us girls dream about; mingling with celebrities, booking modeling jobs, and living it up in The Big Apple (New York City.) Yet, beneath it all, she knew something was missing...

Crown of Beauty: So first of all, tell us how you got involved with the modeling industry. Has this always been a dream of yours?

Rachel: It wasn't really a dream as much as it was a situation of "right place, right time." I had been involved in pageants and had just competed in the Miss Teen USA pageant as Miss North Carolina Teen. I went on to compete in a similar competition, but this time for a potential modeling contract. I won the competition and had a decision to make: college or modeling? I decided to take a shot at New York City in the modeling industry, as I could always return to college when my time was up in the fashion world.

COB: Growing up us as a young girl, what were the "beauty" dynamics like in your family? And by that I mean, did your Mom have a passion for fashion, wear makeup and teach you how to get all dolled up? Or was morning makeup prep-time not something learned from your Mom?

Rachel: My mom had won her High School beauty pageant. I started participating in pageants, earning scholarships and savings bonds, when I was 10. It was a good thing for me, because I had always been a tomboy. Pageants definitely helped me learn to conduct a proper interview, speak well on stage and present myself as a young lady among mayors, girl scouts, or at any number of events raising support for charity or my platform.

COB: Were your parents supportive of your dream to become a model?

Rachel: My father passed away when I was 14, but he did support me in pageants, as well as my mother. When I got the opportunity to move to NYC at 18, my mom was supportive, but not until she made the trek with me—to meet my agents, see where I would live, and gain some understanding of how the industry worked.

COB: As a young girl heading into her teen years, did you struggle to feel beautiful most of the time? Why or why not?

Rachel: I didn't always think of myself as "wonderfully made." Typical? Yes. But wonderful? No. I was a gangly child with extra-long limbs. Second tallest in my sixth grade class including the boys. My knees were knobby and huge, and I weighed 87 pounds and was 5'7". I had numerous nicknames including beanpole and toothpick. This is probably why pageants helped with my self-esteem. Tall and skinny seemed to be a good fit for that industry. But true beauty wasn't something I found right away, it didn't really come until I was 19 and found a relationship with Christ. I finally stopped listening to the negativity in my head and started listening to what He said about me. I was wonderfully made.

COB: How did you find Jesus Christ and start to develop a relationship with Him? Obviously, once you started a relationship with God, your thoughts started to change about certain topics. Two of them being beauty and modesty! Tell us about that.

Rachel: My senior year of high school, when most girls are preparing to launch into college, I was shuttling back and forth from my home in North Carolina to New York City to model for magazines.

I had grown up going to church but never truly accepted Christ as Lord. Sure, I walked an aisle and was baptized, but I spent my life managing to fit God in when and where I wanted Him. In high school, I spent more time trying to blend in to my friends' world than I did trying to stand out. I swore like they did. I laughed at and even told obscene jokes. I harassed unpopular kids. I had conflicts with other girls. I gossiped, lied, and cheated occasionally on my homework—schoolwork wasn't as much of a priority as pageants or cheerleading was. I almost always had a steady boyfriend, and often my identity was wrapped up in him and our impure relationship. Like most people I knew, I went to church. But I juggled being "Christian" on Sunday or at youth camp, disregarding the things of God the rest of the week.

After graduating—and with contract in hand—I moved to New York in hopes of "making it big." I was eighteen and had an apartment in Queens with three other girls. Eventually, out of pride, I convinced myself that I didn't need to be in Queens but in Manhattan where real models live.

At first I thought I was living a life of freedom—doing anything I wished without having to report my activities to anyone or without having to ask permission to do anything I wanted to do. I had my own downtown apartment in New York City; and I was mingling with celebrities and going to parties and prime-time sporting events.

I thought I had the world by the tail, but it had me. I was full of pride. I was going places I shouldn't have been going, doing things I shouldn't have been doing with people I shouldn't have been with. My language was filthy, my wardrobe was degrading, my music was ungodly, and my relationships were toxic.

Everything on the outside looked fine, but on the inside I was miserable and empty. In the still of the night, my heart ached for a relationship with the Jesus that I learned about as a child. I remembered half-heartedly making a decision to follow Jesus years before, but of course, my choices did not reflect that I was born again.

Although I would not admit it at the time, God's love for me poured out as He intervened and began taking things out of my life that were separating me from Him. I started gaining weight, my skin began to break out, bookings were few and far between, and my bank account began to dwindle. Refusing to let God have His way, I went to work at a bar to make ends meet. Bulimia and exercise became routine. But God wasn't finished. He wasn't going to leave me where I was.

On a rare booking, I met two Christian models who shared similar stories of running from or questioning God. Their transparency comforted me. They encouraged me to confess my doubts to God and tell Him I was searching for truth. I ached for what they had.

Desperate for more, I went to a popular Bible-believing church to get counsel from a pastor. As I confessed everything to him, he steered me back to Scripture with nurturing words. Just as the two models had, he urged me to get honest with God.

It took me getting honest with myself before I was able to get honest with God. I came to the place where I realized that I didn't deserve God's favor or His heaven. I read John 3 and Romans 6:23 over and over. I was a sinner and a hypocrite. But it was the best realization I could have had—after all, a person can't be found if he doesn't know he is lost. So, as a broken, humbled nineteen-year-old, I prayed to receive this gift of God—to be born again—and He changed the course of my life forever.

My life as a professional model had new purpose: My industry became my ministry. I shared Christ on castings and bookings with models, makeup artists and photographers. Many seeds were planted and some received Jesus as Savior. Feeling God tug on my heart about leaving the business to attend Bible College, I obeyed, expecting never to re-enter the field of fashion again.

The Bible says in Isaiah 55:9, "As the heavens are higher than the earth, so are my ways higher than your ways and my thoughts than your thoughts." I know this is true because I never expected Him to call me back into the industry.

I've been modeling professionally now for more than 20 years. God has used this business to teach me truths from His Word and has given me a platform to share these truths all over the world—in and out of the fashion industry.

COB: Tell us a little about modesty. Your book, *Fashioned by Faith*, covers this topic in great depth, but if you were to just share one golden nugget of advice about modesty, and why girls should dress modestly, what would you say?

Rachel: Modesty is a way for us to express our integrity in the way we dress. Specifically, by avoiding tight-fitting clothes and those that lack coverage. There are scores of ramifications brought on by immodesty, and I have seen the research (behind it). Eating disorders, low self-esteem, depression, and a bad reputation just to name a few.

COB: You are an amazing example of how a young woman can be both trendy and modest at the same time! Is there a specific product or clothing item in your closet that helps you pull this whole modesty thing off in style? What are some items that every girl should have?

Rachel: I have some basic standards, yes, but the key is creativity—which of course is at the crux of fashion. But the way to pulling it all off is realizing the importance of modesty in the first place so not to be derailed by the latest fashion. Second is using the tool of layering. Whether it be a scarf to cover some cleavage or a layering tank to hide an exposed middle. Knowing the objective and the solutions is how to make it work and make it look great in the process!

COB: Something I personally admire about you is the fact that you dare to combine two very seemingly "opposite" topics like fashion and faith, or modesty and modeling! Surely you've gotten some negative responses about your desire to restore the things of this world, and take them back for the Kingdom of God. What is the hardest thing you've faced in doing this? It must be hard to stand up against popular opinions about these issues in both the world and the church! Any stories to share about that?

Rachel: Haha, many. But one that quickly came to mind is when I was working in Athens, Greece. The outfit was a pair of silver pants and a sheer white top. I took one look at the shirt and wondered where the rest of it was. Realizing I had received the total ensemble, I proceeded to the dressing room.

When I returned, the wardrobe stylist said she could see my bra through the top, and I should take it—my bra—off. Just to show her it was too sheer, I did. I went back into the dressing room and removed my bra. I peeked out to make sure the male photographer wasn't around then exited the room. I knew for sure she would agree the shirt was entirely too sheer to be worn alone. Imagine my surprise when she loved the look and told me to go to the set! I didn't move and told her I would not wear it this way. She said in broken English, "Bra no good, but no bra, okay." Without saying another word, I turned and went back to my dressing area. I took the top off, hung it on its hanger, and carried it out to her. When she saw me, she yelled at me in half Greek, half English to put the top back on and get to the set. I shoved the wrinkled top into her hands and without thinking, replied emphatically, "You wear it!"

I was furious and unafraid of the stylist, and she knew it. As I gathered my things to leave, the British makeup artist intervened. "You can wear it with something underneath if it makes you more comfortable." The stylist left the room without a response and never returned. So, having made my point, I returned to the dressing room.

Sure, it would have been easier to go with the flow and shoot the top (sheer as it was) how they wanted it. And chances are, no one in America would have seen it. But my Father would have seen it. I heard once that character is who you are when no one is looking. In this case, we can add, "when no one from America is looking."

COB: What advice do you have for a girl who wants to go into modeling? How can she keep her heart pure and focused on Christ, while still having fun with the clothes and all the fun, girly things?

Rachel: Well, first of all, it's a very cutthroat business. It's definitely not all fun and games. And unfortunately, it destroys a lot of women. I wouldn't be in the industry if I didn't believe God had called me back into it after Bible College. Even then - believing I was prepared spiritually and emotionally to handle the stress related to the industry, ithas been extremely hard at times. The key for me has been holding it loosely. I've been willing to hang it up and walk away from it if at any point I felt God wanted my career to end. That's the advice I'd give another, hold it loosely. (For information about modeling or industry standards, please visit my website www.modelingchrist.com)

COB: And now for the last question...how do you define true beauty?

Rachel: The standard of the supermodel has changed throughout the years. It began with the rise of the voluptuous Marilyn Monroe. Back then thick hips and a large bust were considered perfection for the iconic woman. In the 60's the trend changed to the boyish hip-less body style of models like Twiggy (who actually wanted to look like Marilyn!)

In the 80's the term supermodel was introduced, and with it curvy, toned women like Cindy Crawford and Claudia Schiffer. But as the 90's approached, Kate Moss brought back the waif and ultra-thin models, and flat chests were the trend. Today, a size 10-12 is considered plus-size in the modeling industry, but the average American woman is 5'4" and wears a size 14!

The point is, whether you're tall, thin, curvy, or boney, you're always going to compare yourself to someone else unless you embrace who you are. The only standard for greatness is to love yourself from the inside, out. I wasn't able to do that until I found my identity in Jesus Christ instead of the image in my mirror.

"Instead, it should be that of your inner self; the unfading beauty of a gentle and quiet spirit which is of great worth in God's sight." 1 Peter 3:4

~*~

Rachel Lee Carter is a professional model, speaker, Bible teacher, and author of *Fashioned by Faith*. Be sure to check out her book which sheds light on trends, true beauty, modesty and more. Perfect for youth leaders, teen girls, and small group encouragement!

You Might Be Single And Homeschooled If...

-You've experienced the true struggle of putting an adorable outfit back on the rack at your favorite store, because it doesn't meet your modesty standards and might tempt a brother in Christ.

-"Date night" at your house means spending one-on-one time with Mom and Dad.

-Your idea of the perfect relationship is Missy and Willie from the *Love Comes Softly* series.

-*Barlow Girl* inspired you to get a purity ring and made waiting "cool."

-Your Dad always says jokingly (with undertones of seriousness), "You're not allowed to date until you're married!"

-You already write love letters to your future husband.

-The boys of *One Direction* are the only males in your life that have ever told you, "You're beautiful!" (Besides your Dad, of course.)

-Your first kiss won't happen until your wedding day.

-You daydream about marrying a Duggar boy.

-Your first crush was Gilbert from *Little House on the Prairie*.

-Your idea of a dream proposal is one at Disney World.

-If someone asks you what the definition of true love is, you reply, "Cory and Topenga."

-You can't wait to be a bridesmaid at your best friend's wedding.

-Sometimes you wonder if there's something wrong with you because nobody has ever asked you out!

-Old-school Taylor Swift music describes your perfect love life (if you had one).

-You secretly hope that you will marry someone who loves classic musicals and Disney movies as much as you do.

-You kinda want to marry a guy like Flynn Rider. (Yes, you're in love with a cartoon character.)

-You pray for your future husband all the time.

-You refer to your future man as "Boaz."

-You know you're not going to have a small wedding because your family is so big!

-Whenever you go to *Winter Jam*, you secretly keep your eyes peeled for "the one!"

-You want to marry Josh Hutcherson but know the chances of that happening are next to impossible.

-The day Jill Duggar got married became a national holiday at your house!

-There's nothing more attractive about a guy than watching him passionately worship the Lord.

-Or when a guy runs around playing with little kids.

-"And We Haven't Even Kissed," by Moriah Peters, is your love story anthem.

-You refer to immature guys as "Frogs", thanks to *Superchick*.

-Every Thanksgiving your extended family makes jokes about your wedding day, seriously doubting that will ever happen, and asking about your non-existent boyfriend.

-All of your friends' moms, sweet old ladies at the grocery store, and even your pastor's wife tell you how beautiful you are...but sometimes you doubt their words, because no guy has ever expressed much interest in you.

-You think the Lord told you that you might be the next Mrs. Tim Tebow.

-You and all your friends have nicknames for your non-existent boyfriends.

-While the world is out dating and partying it up, Friday nights are usually spent with your favorite book.

-You already have your whole wedding planned out on Pinterest. (Don't lie.)

-Your parents always joke about finding you a husband at the next big homeschool convention.

-You daydream about going on a mission trip and meeting the love of your life.

-There's so much relationship drama that happens at your youth group, it's hard to keep up.

-On Valentine's Day, you wish everyone, "Happy Singles Awareness Day!"

-Every *Blimey Cow* video about relationships pretty much describes your life.

-You use funny phrases that the world might not understand, like "Kingdom joining," "courtship," and "purity".

-You love the idea of marrying a youth pastor.

-The majority of your crushes are fictional characters in books, and you find them to be much more amazing than the guys you know in real life.

-You just read through this list and thought, "That is so me!"

~*~

Boy Advice From The Pros

Over the years, Crown of Beauty Magazine has done dozens of interviews. We've asked a lot of people for boy and relationship advice, but these answers were our absolute favorites!

Jessa Duggar Seewald: I think the tendency often is to look just at the outward appearance. And that's where you can be fooled. Because girls want the cute guy, you know? And sometimes they just look at that, and only go off looks. Or sometimes it can be his personality, and they think, 'Oh, he has a great sense of humor, he makes me laugh. Oh, that's nice, I like laughing, I like feeling happy and being joyful, so he must be a good guy.' And they don't really look for character qualities in his life.

So in our book {*Growing Up Duggar*} we encourage girls to look beyond that and not just say, 'Oh, he's super cute!' Or, 'He makes me happy,' but ask yourself, 'Is he full of Godly character? Is he honest? Is he hard working? Is he self-controlled? Is he slow to anger?

That's a huge thing because a lot of guys, when they're at a sporting event and their team doesn't win, they just fly off the handle in rage. And that's not something you want as a husband, a man, as the father of your children. Ask yourself this question to decide: 'Is this a man that I would like to spend the rest of my life with?' And also getting to know him in an environment where he's spending a lot of time in already, whether that be with his family or otherwise, so that you're not only going on dates within the perfect environment or the perfect setting, but really seeing what he's like in real life situations, and spending time together with his family, or whatever that may look like.

~*~

Moriah Peters and Joel Smallbone:

Moriah: I was dating the man who is now my husband. We were sitting on the couch watching *Young Victoria*. I sat there realizing that we could sit there and not be tempted to kiss or have any physical contact. We could just have fun without getting physical. I had made a promise to save my first kiss for my wedding day (more on that in a little bit), so I made sure that my significant others knew that. Anyway Joel and I were watching a movie. Then this song hit me like a ton of bricks. I excused myself to go record this song that just came to me, before I went back to the couch and finished watching the movie.

When I had my first kiss on my wedding day, you can't imagine how good it felt. It was like happiness, gladness, joy, and peace rushing through me. Happiness because God ignored my teenage prayers asking for a boyfriend when I was like twelve, and happiness because He answered my prayers for a man who would love Him more than he would love me. I felt gladness because I saved myself for the one I would spend the rest of my days with, and gladness because I didn't give in to temptation. I experienced joy because the day finally came. I had joy because my Jesus picked the perfect guy for me. I had peace because I knew that God was always taking care of me. He saw the big picture when I didn't.

I just really want to encourage girls. If you know that you've gone farther than you should've in a relationship, it is okay. God will forgive you. He died on the cross to wipe your sins white as snow. Because of His blood we are white. If you haven't kissed yet, take heart. The day when you say 'I do' and promise yourself to your husband until the day that you are separated by death, the feeling that you will get shall be one of the most wonderful feelings you've ever felt.

Girls, in the end, I just really want to let you know that God has everything in control. Don't force yourself into a relationship that isn't ready to be opened up yet. All good things come from patience.

Crown of Beauty: Why don't you start by telling us about how you met your spouse, giving us a little look inside the backside of your love story?

Joel: I first met Moriah at my brother Luke's wedding. He had invited a mutual friend. The card said. "you and one guest."
So, my friend decided that he would bring Moriah for the specific purpose of introducing the two of us to each other. I had not planned on meeting anyone special at the wedding. I actually had, earlier that week, just come to rest with the fact that God had me single for a reason. I thought that I would know everyone at the wedding then I turn around and see this beautiful young lady standing there. I was simply

dumbfounded; the classic foot-in-mouth disease. I left my brother's wedding on June 26th, 2010, thinking that I just met the woman that I was going to marry. Then we dated for about two years, got engaged, and here we stand today.

Moriah: Neither of us anticipated meeting anyone special that night and both of us had just come to peace with our singleness. That being said, he was rather shocked upon first meeting and I was rather rude! I wish I could tell it differently but I simply didn't want to stroke his ego; however, after spending a few days writing a song together ("I'll Wait for You, Love") I learned that he was one of the most humble men I'd ever met.

COB: If a couple who recently started courting (dating with a purpose) came to you and asked for advice on how to center their relationship around God, what advice would you give them?

Joel: I would tell them that a relationship starts with having a real and honest connection with God. Pray together. The thing I've learned, whether it be a spiritual relationship, a dating relationship, or a friend relationship, is that the health of a relationship is based on how often you communicate with one another. And how you love and cherish one another. All those rules apply to dating, but they also apply to our relationship with God. We can't expect to have a flourishing relationship with God if we never talk to Him. You have to want to grow and want to know Him. Before the sun rises, seek Him in the morning.

Moriah: Communicate honestly with God, each other and a mentor. Joel and I found that we were best able to communicate with one another if we were having personal time with God first. Be honest with someone you admire and trust about your struggles. It's easy to fall into guilt when you cross a line in relationship, but that only leads us to shame. God wants us to come to Him and openly communicate our faults, so that they lose their power over us.

Joel: Guys can encourage girls in this society that we live in, that is focused on body image, looks, beauty, and physicality. I think that a man can encourage a woman by focusing on the heart, by focusing on who the girl is, and not what the girl looks like or what the girl does. Really focus on who the girl is as a person; finding the most beautiful aspect of her character. Not only verbal words, but when a guy actually takes action it speaks to girls. Girls, I can't speak for all men because everyone is unique and different, but when I feel most loved and cherished by my wife is when she shows me that she cares.

Moriah: Girls, I pray that we would know our worth and wait for a man who would recognize that value. How can we encourage our brothers to see us the way God sees us if we don't gain His perspective first? Men, as you make knowing Christ your aim, He will begin to give you His eyes for his daughters. Respect and serve every woman that comes in your path the way that Jesus did and does.

~*~

Kari Jobe:
Only dive in if you know you have peace from the Lord and guard your heart until you know He's God's guy for you. Allow God to show you who the guy really is; don't create an idea of who you think the guy is. You want to marry someone you know, not who you think you know.

COB: It's been so much fun watching your love story unfold with Cody. But let's return to the beginning, long before Cody even came into the picture. What caused you to hand the pen of your love story over to God and let Him be the Author?

Kari: I grew up in a Christian home with a wonderful mom and dad. I have always known that God would help me know when the right man had come into my life. I dated a few different guys while growing up and would have a lack of peace about marriage, and so I would end my relationship quite often. I knew that it would be important for me to marry someone who had the same passions as me and felt called to similar things. That helped me stay focused on waiting on God's best for me.

COB: While you were waiting for your husband, did you ever get discouraged? If so, what encouraged you the most when you felt like the wait was getting too long?

Kari: I got discouraged each time I had to break off a relationship with boys in the past, but I had to follow where the peace was, and I never quite had it until Cody. I've always tried to surround myself with solid friends and mentors. I think it's what consistently kept me on track to wait for God's man for me.

COB: How did you guys meet? What happened? Did sparks fly right away? Or was it more of a gradual process of getting to know one another?

Kari: Cody and I met at church years ago. I was looking for an acoustic guitar player and singer to travel with me. We were just really good friends for a few years without any actual romantic feelings for each other. Those came about four years after building a friendship. I love that it happened this way because it's really special to marry your best friend. Someone you know really well and who is passionate about many of the same things you are. I didn't have to try and get to know him once we were married, and there's a comfort in that.

COB: How did you know that Cody was the one God had chosen for you?

Kari: I had peace to my very core. As I took a step back and looked at our callings, paths, and passions I just really knew that we seemed perfect for each other. His pursuit of me caused me to fall for him as well. He swept me off my feet. (Insert girls saying "Awww"... haha)

COB: As a married woman, if you could go back and tell your single self something and offer a piece of advice, what would you say?

Kari: I would tell myself to have a ton more friends and hang with groups, because you really get to know people a lot easier in groups. I would have done a lot better job guarding my young heart. It's really hard to heal from a broken heart.

~.*~.

Jill Duggar Dillard: When I was young, my parents really encouraged me not to focus on marriage as being the 'solve all,' but to focus on my relationship with God. So that really is what encouraged me as a young

person, to know that God was to bring that person into my life, in His timing. And as long as you're seeking Him, He'll make that happen. A lot of times, as a young girl I would think,
"Well, what about that guy...or what about that guy?"

But my parents would be steadfast in encouraging me to say, "What kind of girl is a Godly guy looking for?" He's not looking for somebody who's out looking at all the other guys, wondering "Is this the one?!" Not someone who is trying out his last name and planning out her wedding colors and all that! He's looking for somebody who's focused and driven, and who has priorities and goals that are eternal.

So that's something my parents would say over and over to my sisters and me, and to my brothers; to focus on Christ, and God will make everything else come in His timing. So as a young girl I was inspired by different friends of mine that I saw go through the courtship process, and I knew that's what I wanted to do. I didn't want to give pieces of my heart away. I really wanted to save myself for the one that God would have for me.

COB: So was waiting a difficult thing for you? Or was it easy, because of how you've been raised and because of what your parents instilled in you at such a young age?

Jill: No, it wasn't easy! For everybody, it doesn't matter what background you come from, you want to be married and you have desires that God places in your heart for a reason. So it's not like you're immune to those feelings just because you choose a different route. There were times when I was wondering, "Am I ever going to get married?" You can be sixteen and wonder that! You're not immune to it!

COB: So what did you do to encourage yourself when you got down in the dumps about being single?

Jill: My parents encouraged me to create a list of character qualities that I was looking for in my future spouse (which I wrote in the back of my journal), and also to pray for my future spouse. At times when I was struggling in my thinking about guys, and I needed to NOT be thinking in that direction, I would shift my focus and really focus in on the Lord. But when I needed to be thinking about them, and I needed to focus on them in a positive way, I would write this list in the back of my journal. And I wasn't really faithful to journal all the time, but I would write down character qualities that I wanted in a future husband. Just different things that I saw in Godly men that I admired, like in preachers, or different things that I might see and think, "Oh that is a really good quality that is essential in a husband!" Or, on the flip side, thinking about character qualities or lack thereof, that you don't want in a future spouse.

So I wrote both those things in the back of my journal, and sometimes I would write scripture verses next to them, like warnings from Proverbs, and just practical things. So then when it came to my courtship with Derick, I was able to pull my list out and ask him about these things.

And not just character qualities, but also "What do you believe about this," or "what do you believe about that?" So that was huge! That was really helpful for me, even in focusing as a young girl. So when I saw someone, I would think, "That's not the right one for me," or "It's not God's timing," because they don't have those character qualities.

Now you're not looking for somebody who's perfect, but you're looking for somebody who's aspiring to follow Christ and work in those areas.

Sometimes I would ask Derick a question about something when we were getting to know each other, and he may not have had the answer. I would say, "What do you think about this in Scripture?" And maybe I didn't really know what I thought about it either and was still studying it, but I wanted to know where he stood. He might say, "I'm not sure. But I would like to research that." And that's okay! You don't want to marry somebody who is a know-it-all!

COB: When you chose to hand God the pen of your life, and allowed Him to write out His story for you and Derick, did you ever imagine that things would unfold the way they did?

Jill: Oh no, I was like totally surprised at what God did with our love story! You know, I've always imagined that I would probably know the guy for awhile, kind of get to know him, see how it works out, and then go from there. I thought we might live in the same area, or maybe he would be from somewhere far, but we would at least get to know each other for awhile. Well God had different plans there! I told this to my friends too, who were like, "Are you crazy?! You're going across the world to meet this guy?!"

COB: Jill explained how she could see the benefits of their unique story, and how it helped her to grow on a personal level in her walk with God...

Jill: I think it was very much beneficial that our relationship was different, because it forced me to ask tough questions at the beginning, and not just get to know each other on a social level. What people do a lot of times these days is they just hang out and then yeah, maybe you get to see how they react at a basketball game or football game or something like that (which is important too), but you get to know each other then on a really surface level. And then when you think, "Hey, we might like each other," then you start deeper. But with Derick and I, I feel like it was God's protection; it was good that we were able to ask those tough questions from the get-go. I would encourage all young ladies in this. I had a friend the other day who said she's courting now, and was asking advice, and I said, "Communication!" Communicate. It's huge.

But it's like throwing up; you feel horrible asking all these (hard) questions, but you feel much better afterward. You want to get those things out there. You don't want to wait three or six months down the road, get more connected, have more ties, and then realize, "Oh goodness, he doesn't believe the same way I do about this," or "We can't get married because of this or that," or whatever, just because you finally got the guts to ask him those questions. So it's good to communicate about those types of things early on.

~*~

PART 4: CHANGING THE WORLD

Shattering My Tea Cup of Comfort

Comfort. It's such a sweet word. Our toes tingle and hearts sigh just at the mention of it. I adore comfort. There's nothing like putting on my favorite fuzzy socks, warming my fingers with a cup of tea, and cuddling up with my laptop on the sofa. Certain sounds, sights, and smells release the power of sweet nostalgia, and quickly usher me into a state of pure bliss. Homemade bread, baking in the oven. The white background noise of *Monday Night Football*. Raindrops gently dancing on my rooftop. Cushioned pews at church. Taco night. The inexpressible joys of discovering treasures on Pinterest.

Ahh, this life is so comfortable.

Every once in a while my creamy, marshmallow-y hot chocolate cup of life is bombarded by a foreign invader. I gasp in sheer horror as pain and discomfort attempt to mess up the soundtrack of my perfect little life. The Wi-Fi connection drops. My texts won't go through! I can't use the internet for days. The electricity goes out. I can no longer watch reruns of *Boy Meets World*. The microwave oven blows up. No more insta-popcorn. Church runs a little bit too long, and my stomach is growling. I'm crabby because there's "no food in the house!" I complain about the annoying chick at work who doesn't seem to like Christians. I don't want to lift weights anymore because my tiny little arms hurt soooo badly afterward. Don't ask me to spend my Tuesday evening at the local outreach center feeding the homeless....because, well....then I'll miss the next episode of *19 Kids and Counting*. Does God really want me to spend my birthday money to feed those who are starving in another country? What about that expensive new pair of boots that I want?!

If any of the scenarios above sound familiar, you've probably tweeted about them and then added the hashtag #FirstWorldProbs.

You guys, let's be real. Sometimes we are such wimps. (Now before you toss this book out the window and gasp in offense, "Did she just call me a wimp?!" Allow me to explain.)

Let me tell you a little story. One day, as I was skipping through the grassy fields of my sugar-sweet life, I saw an image that didn't sit well with me. It was so graphically horrific that I literally felt sick to my stomach. There, blinking on the computer screen in front of my eyes, lay the picture of a little girl who was freshly beheaded.

I did a double take, my eyes struggling to process the staggering sight. She couldn't have been any older than four or five. Her sweet little stocking-footed toes lay lifeless, and the little girl in her dress looked as if she should be out playing imaginary games with her dolls. But she wasn't. Because she had no head. Yes, there was blood. And yes, I felt a little queasy, but the most powerful emotion ruling in my heart at that moment was absolute outrage.

Why?

Because I wasn't leafing through a history book. This wasn't something that took place years ago. No, my sisters, this was just last week. Photograph after photograph spoke of the bloody atrocity. Christians in Iraq and Syria are being systematically hunted down, and murdered. Men are being crucified, and women are watching their children die before their very eyes. Simply because they won't succumb to the fear and deny that Jesus Christ is Lord.

Talk about an *uncomfortable* situation.

Why do I get so frustrated when my cell phone charger won't work? Why do I find myself whimpering and complaining every time I face a challenging situation?

My dear sisters, the Lord Jesus is calling out to us. He desires to shake us and awaken us. We are living in a hazy dream world, stumbling around, subscribing to the culture around us. We obsess over makeup, bad hair days, Hollywood celebrities, and the latest gossip at school...meanwhile our brothers and sisters in Christ are being murdered for the same faith that we profess in total freedom and safety.

Isaiah 51:2 says, "Awake, awake O Zion! Clothe yourself with strength! Put on your garments of splendor..." Can you hear the rumblings of His Spirit inside of you? Can you hear the whisper of His heartbeat? He is calling you to arise! What is it that He desires to express through your life, and let His message roar out of you like an unstoppable lion? Jesus said, "That which is whispered in your ear, proclaim it from the rooftops." [Matthew 10:27]. What is it that God has been speaking to your soul? What does He desire to awaken you to?

As God's chosen generation [1 Peter 2:9], He is calling us to clothe ourselves with strength! I cannot afford for my faith to be a soft and squeezable plush toy. I must rise as the Queen He has called me to be [Esther 4:14] and allow Him to strengthen every last inch of my heart!

What if persecution like this comes to the United States? What if famine or severe hunger strikes? Will my faith hold up then? Who will my unshakable and unwavering trust be built upon then?

We cannot be casual about our relationships with Jesus. Casual Christianity is not what God requires of us. He says, "Whoever wants to be my disciple must deny themselves and take up their cross and follow me." [Matthew 16:27]

Princess, you are called to be a brave and fearless warrior for the Kingdom of Heaven. God did not save you to hide you in a tower of luxury and comfort, then stand back and say, "There! Now stay inside your soft little bubble, and don't let the devil getcha!"

While it is true that you may have been tucked away for a season of time in your life, to undergo required training and important princess lessons, the time for sitting around is no more. Little Miss Muffet needs to get up off her tuffet!

Within these pages you will meet many princess warriors who have stepped out of their comfy surroundings and embarked on a most frightful, yet glorious mission. You will meet young women [and men] who are lifting up their swords, and letting out a battle cry. Just like Queen Susan from the Chronicles of Narnia, we have been chosen to march into the enemy's camp, to bring freedom to the captives. With *The Dreamers Issue* it was our prayer to inspire you and let your heart soar as high and as far as it could. God's Kingdom is full of daydreamers. We have such amazing visions that God has planted inside of our hearts. But quite often, He is waiting on us to make the first move, in order to see these dreams become a reality on the earth.

The Mission Issue is all about mobilizing you. The call to action has been clearly proclaimed, but it is high time that we rise up and do something about it!

It is my prayer that by the time you reach the end of this issue (hey, maybe even by the time you finish reading this article!) your heart will be so stirred by God's Holy Spirit, that a fiery resolve of steel will be set in your soul. My prayer is that you set your heart like flint and run passionately after the Lord, seeking Him like you never have before. He is calling us to be radical. He is calling us to go to the ends of the earth and proclaim His name. He is calling each of us to a totally unique, one of a kind mission field. It is your responsibility to tend to that field, plant seeds, and bring in the harvest when it sprouts up!

The Lord desires to do SO much on this earth before the final curtain call, when He returns for His Bride, the Church, but He needs us to move!

I try not to frown when Christians say things like, "Why do bad things happen to good people? Why are poor, dirty, and hungry kids starving to death every day? Why is there human trafficking? Why is Hollywood so messed up? Why are there school shootings? Why is there so much bullying?"

We pray, and beg, and ask God to change these things, yet we fail to realize that He has put us on this earth so that we can change them! He has given us everything we need; the tools, the armor, the Sword of the Spirit [His Holy Word], and the supernatural empowerment of His Holy Spirit living in us.

What more could a girl ask for?! Isn't it time that we dive into the amazing painting that God is creating, rather than sit around and wait to see how the picture is going to turn out?

You are a brush stroke in His hand. Surrender to what the Master Artist wants to use you to create!

If you feel like you're not exactly sure where your Mission Field is, or know what God has called you to do on this earth, that's okay! This issue is loaded with ideas! You don't need to wait for the perfect thing to fall out of Heaven and hit you on the head. Just pick something! If you like one of the ideas that you read about in this issue, go for it! Be faithful with the little, and He will guide you into all truth. He will show you, in time, where exactly it is that He wants you to be. He promises to guide your steps. But you have to start walking in a general direction before He can guide you! I promise that there is absolutely something that you can do to change this world. Don't be left on the sidelines. The moment you've been waiting for all your life...it's here. It's right now. Your moment of opportunity is today. Not tomorrow, not when you graduate High School, not when you get married. The hour has arrived. Our time is now.

~*~

Getting Out of the Shire

I'll never forget the first time I saw a sea of sparkling glow sticks, waving in the dark at a Taylor Swift concert. Illuminated like electric jellyfish, every excited fan held high an emblem of light in the ocean of excitement.

I felt my stomach do several flip-flops, as I realized I was gnawing on my fingernails. I was so nervous for her! I imagined what it might be like to step solo onto a stage where thousands of twinkling eyes watched your every move, and I was so anxious!

The roar of bottled-up energy exploded when Taylor walked onstage, burst through my television set, and made me feel as if I were there. In that moment, I knew my story would be similar to Taylor's. The tale of an unsuspecting underdog who takes over the world.

Just like Miss Swift, I have always been a dreamer. If you're not familiar with Taylor's story, and all you see is her sparkly dresses and armloads of CMA awards, it may be easy to roll your eyes and think, "What did she do to reach such success?" Maybe a better question to ask yourself is, "What didn't she do?" She sacrificed precious social time to attend songwriting classes, knocked on every door in Music Row, played guitar for unthinkable hours, and perhaps most importantly...she believed in her dreams. The vision of playing her music to sold out stadiums consumed her thoughts until they had no choice but to turn into reality. She believed she was a superstar long before anyone else did.

In the same way, my imagination daily carries me to far off, radical scenarios. My heart travels and lingers in such glorious places, in which practical common sense would scold and arrest me for thinking so BIG. My toughest critics (doubt, fear, and the opinions of those around me) attempt to shoot fiery darts at my wildest dreams. Doubt says it will never happen, fear whispers all the ways I could fail, and worrying about what other people think can keep my mouth shut tight. If I'm not careful, I could let these dreams lie dormant for years, locked in a cage, the doors sealed with an icy layer of frozen insecurity.

There was a time in my life a few years ago, when I was afraid to open my mouth and speak about my dreams. Sure, I would tell people the realistic things, the un-laughable, practical things...but I kept my deepest desires to myself, pretty confident that my friends would think I was NUTS.

I never told anyone that I wanted my life to influence millions, to start my own magazine and TV show, record an album, go on tour, write books, build orphanages, take busloads of underprivileged kids to Disney World, own a library and an ice cream parlor, and open a school.

When extended family members asked me what I planned on doing after graduating high school, my eyes grew wide with fear. What in the world was I going to tell them?!

After seeing Joseph's example in the Bible, I figured I should keep my lips zipped. (When Joseph told his brothers about his prophetic dream, that he would one day be their ruler, they "despised Joseph, and hated him all the more." Gen. 37:5.)

There came a time in my life when I had a choice to make. If I refused to confront fear and embrace my impossible dreams, I might have ended up like those folks who wait until retirement to do what they've wanted to do their whole lives. If I ignored my dreams and never let them blossom for fear of what might happen if they burst out of control...my heart might have become ill.

Proverbs 13:12, "A desire fulfilled is a tree of life, but hope deferred makes the heart sick."

There are too many sick, depressed hearts walking around, wishing they could make a move and pursue the life they've always hoped for, but are too afraid to do it.

Imagine the horror if Cinderella never left her home for fear that she wasn't good enough to be a royal. What a tragic ending to her story. What if Walt Disney never sketched his first mouse, despising such meager beginnings? What if Bethany Hamilton (a pro surfer whose arm got ripped off by a shark) never got back in the water because of fear that something horrible might happen again? If any of these dreamers had ignored what their hearts longed to do, settled down and got a "regular" job, their spirits would have been crushed.

Every human has a choice. We can choose to pursue our dreams, set out on wild and wonderful adventures, slay giants, conquer fear, and fulfill our destines. OR, we can hide, tucked away; sitting in our little house of tiny mindsets, clinging to our hankies of control and obsessing over our mother's fine dish set, insisting on the old way of life. Like The Hobbit, sometimes we are afraid to step out the front door of our comfort zone, expand our territory, and set out on a real adventure.

Someone once said, "You can either fall off the couch and die. Or you can go mountain climbing and die." A little dramatic, I know, but the case is made. Isaiah 54:2-3 says: "Enlarge the place of your tent, and let them stretch out the curtains of your dwellings; do not spare; lengthen your cords, strengthen your stakes. For you shall expand to the right and to the left..."

In 1 Chronicles 4:10, Jabez cried out to the Lord, "Oh that you would bless me and expand my territory!" Jabez was counted among the crazy dreamers. He wasn't going to settle for life in a Hobbit hole, living a small, average existence. Jabez knew he needed to be stretched out, expanded, lengthened, and strengthened, like every dreamer does. And so, he prayed for mental enlargement. He prayed for courage to get out of the Shire.

"Ptsh, well that's a selfish prayer," one might say. "We need to be content with our lives, and where God has placed us. Don't go asking for more. Maybe God doesn't want your dreams to come true at all."

Hmm...does that sound like our Heavenly Father? Why would He place a desire so deeply within us, something that is woven into our very DNA then deny us the fulfillment of it? A good Father doesn't show his daughter her Christmas presents all wrapped up then throw them in the trash. That would be twisted and evil, and we know that there is no darkness or shifting shadow in God. (Check out James 1:17.) If our blazing hearts' desires are interpreted as evil selfishness that needs to be quenched, and foolishness to be thrown away, then it's no wonder so many people are miserable in this world.

Have we ever paused to ask, "Who gives us these dreams? What causes

the painter to paint, the singer to sing, and the doctor to heal? Who is the Author of these wild notions?"
It is God who works and wills in us, to do good works, which He prepared in advance for us to do (Eph. 2:10) If God is the One who causes our hearts to wake in the morning, and gifts our hearts with the energy to write a book, record an album, feed the hungry, clothe orphans, or create new jewelry designs, doesn't He have something to do with it? Could it be that our dreams are actually His dreams?

Could it be that just like in the *Hobbit*, our comfy little homes of ho-hum life have been bombarded by a calling to go explore? Could it be that the painful, confusing dissatisfaction we experience in our comfort zone of common sense is meant to send us running through the doorway of hapless dreaming, shouting like a lunatic, trampling down every terrifying giant that stands in the way of our destiny?!

Nothing we have is our own. Everything about us comes from our Creator; every good idea, every brilliant invention, and every tender thought of love, to make someone else's life better. He is the Author of love, and the Author of our childhood dreams.

Sister, it's time we get out of the Shire. Adventure is out there. Don't allow big, ugly monsters of doubt, or fire-breathing dragons of man's opinion, to keep you locked up. There is a whole land of adventures, whimsical dreams, and courageous moments awaiting you.

So be brave, and take heart my valiant sister! Take up your Heavenly weapons, and lift high the shield of radical faith. Take the fearless stance of Joshua and remind yourself of these words spoken from Heaven:

"Be strong and very courageous. Do not be afraid, do not be terrified. For the Lord your God is with you wherever you go." (Joshua 1:9) A land of promise is spread out before you. Are you ready to leave the Shire?

~*~

Lindsay's Heartbeat for India

Meet Lindsay. She grew up in Kansas as a pastor's daughter, and has always had a great love for God, and a passion for the local church. But missions was not something on her mind.

"I wish I could say that I grew up with missions on my heart and a desire to one day build orphanages in third-world countries, but that wouldn't be true!" says Lindsay.

Then one day God stepped in and changed her plans. "I met the man who would soon be my husband. He had been doing missions since he was 13, spending many summers of his teenage life in nations I had never even thought of visiting! After meeting, I joined with him and his missions organization (Missions.Me) and went to the Dominican Republic when I was 19. I was hooked after that!"

Lindsay's first trip to India was life changing. "I was completely blindsided!" She explains, "There were street children EVERYWHERE...like someone had let out a school bus after school. They had nowhere to go, except wander the streets. Studies show that the estimated 25 million street children in India end up in 1 of 3 places: forced child labor, sex trafficking, or a life of begging on the streets. That's it! I couldn't go about my life, not even that week, without doing something about it.

When I met a particular group of 50 kids through a pastor friend, my heart was broken. They were so cute, so innocent, and so vulnerable. The oldest of the group wasn't over the age of 12. We decided right then and there to build them a house, not knowing what that would entail! I just knew that these kids needed a home, as soon as humanly possible, to get them off of the streets and into a loving and nurturing environment.

Over the next few months I prayed for vision and direction, and felt like "Angel House" was the perfect name for the project.

The Vision: Angel House
I scribbled down a logo and made a makeshift website, hoping it would gain some traction. I had no idea what was to come!

That December we went back to India and opened our very first Angel House rescue orphanage. We cut the ribbon on that home, and all 50 children ran into the house like it was Disney World! None of these kids had ever slept on a bed or with a pillow in their entire lives. It was the most emotional day of my life!

We knew we couldn't stop there, so with much prayer and amazing people who were supporting us, we committed our lifetime to rescue as many children off the streets as we could. However, we knew it would take many miracles! I was just 23 years old. One month after the opening of the home, my husband and I were praying and asking God to help us with the finances to build more of these homes. We prayed "God, if you will put the money in our hands, we will give it right back to you!" I kid you not, 2 days later I got a call from the Executive Producer of the NBC gameshow Minute To Win It. My best friend had applied for the show and written my name down as a possible partner to play with! The producer said, "So, I have to ask, what would you do if you won the 1 million dollars?" I was delighted as I got to share with her the vision of Angel House and send her the video of the grand opening just 1 month prior. Needless to say, we got on the show, made it to Level 8, split $250,000 between us, and that year 8.5 million households heard about what God was doing through Angel House! In 2011, with that money and the momentum it created, we were able to build 11 Angel Houses!

Since the show, we have steadily had miracle after miracle. The vision is unfolding before our eyes. Something my dad always says is, "Don't ask God to bless what you are doing. Do what God is blessing!" We know we are on the right track, because the blessing of God is all over these projects. This December the Angel House team will cut the ribbon on the 73rd. orphanage since 2010!"

A Typical Day in India?
"A typical day on the mission field is full! Since we usually open multiple homes on each trip, and the trips are 10 days in length, each day is usually dedicated to a new home opening. Most days we get up early, have a devotional during breakfast, and head out either by bus or train to the remote city or village where the new orphanage is located. It is really fun because it truly is a celebration that the entire village has been anticipating for 6 months as they have watched the construction take

place. Everyone wants to come see what's going on! There's usually a lot of music, food, dancing and tears as our team gets to love on these kids all day long. We get to pray over the homes, cut the ribbon, and watch the kids run into the home for the very first time.

It is the best, as you truly witness a miracle! At our homes, we also make sure there is fresh water by installing a fresh water well. This just adds to the celebration, as we let the kids pump the water and the entire village drinks and plays in the water! It really is a joyous celebration.

During the day we lavish the children with gifts consisting of new clothing, backpacks full of school supplies (since each child is now enrolled in local school) and TOYS! We have a blast. Then we wake up and do it all over again!"

Taking Action
Hearing about stories like Lindsay's always inspires me. But it can also cause me to think, "What am I supposed to do with my life? Will I ever make that big of an impact?"

We asked Lindsay how she found her purpose in life: "Before starting Angel House, I always struggled with what my place would be. I had a college degree and I was married, so by most standards, I was doing pretty well! But I always had a stirring that there was more for me. I love that God called me to this at such a young age, because I was totally unqualified. That let me know that HE was taking care of the details, I just needed to walk it out! As I have grown and learned more over the years, it still amazes me that He chose me for this task. Never count yourself out, that's for sure!"

Lindsay's best advice for other world changers out there is to "Learn from someone who is doing what you see yourself doing. I am so lucky that I had friends doing similar works on the mission field, that I could run to when I got overwhelmed! I call that, "finding your Elizabeth." In the Bible, when Mary finds out that she is pregnant supernaturally, it says that she ran to the house of Elizabeth, who was also carrying something supernatural from God — a child in her old age. They had something in common and they stuck together!"

Amazing Memories

"One of my favorite memories was actually at the very first home opening in 2010. There was a little girl named Naveena, and she was one that I had really connected with earlier that year. To come back in December and see her completely different — bathed, healthier and full of life — was an amazing experience. We spent the whole day together, and I didn't know how I was going to leave her! Although I wasn't a mother at the time, I could only imagine how I would feel about my own kids if I loved her that much! She's still special to me, and I enjoy getting photos of her to watch her grow!"

~*~

We are so excited to announce that *Crown of Beauty* is officially partnering with *Angel House Orphan Rescue* to build a home for precious princesses in India!

That's right, we are building an orphanage. Who is we? You. Her. Us. Every girl who reads this book! We've been talking about being world changers, isn't it time for us to stand up in our God-given calling as His princesses, and rescue His royal children?!

With this project you have the opportunity to touch the lives of precious gems on the other side of the ocean, these abandoned children who desperately need our help. Tonight there are children fighting for their lives in the streets, without parents, or even a comfy pillow to rest their little heads on.

I don't know about you, but I am **not okay** with that. So, I'm going to do something about it. And if you're on board for this adventure, then so are you! Let's change these children's lives together!

Donate now by visiting: missions.me/crownofbeautyorphanage
Or to discover fun and creative ways that you can get involved with this project, visit www.crownofbeautymagazine.com

Stop & Go

Windows down. Hair blowing. Breeze flowing. Christian music going. My three little ones are dancing to the music, baby talking, and watching the houses and shops pass by. This is the highlight of a typical week day while our favorite man, sweet Daddy, is working. Recently, while riding, I read this profound statement on a church marquee: "God orders our steps, and God also orders our stops."

"Stop! Wait! It's not quite time. Rest! Take a chill pill, Deanna! Slow down, Honey."

To be quite frank, these words make me go, GRRRRrrr. For years, these suggestions, or commands should I say, would drop tons of irritation into my heart. "Come on people!" I would say, "Life is an adventure! Life is fun on the GO. I like to journey on the fast track. Give me a thrill ride, please. Take me on a roller coaster. Is it extremely fast? I'm there! Downhill! Screammmmm!"

Theme parks are crazy fun, don't you agree?! But let me remind you: all roller coaster rides must come to an end. Otherwise, you will experience much fatigue, dizziness, and become (in my words) "wore-slap-out!" Road trips without rest stops or restrooms would be absolutely miserable. Similarly, as you fulfill your God-given assignment, whether it is through a career, hands-on full-time ministry, or being a stay-at-home-mom, you must learn to slow down, stop, and rest in the sweet presence of Daddy Jesus.

Fill Up on Fuel
Over the past 6 years I have learned that the only way I can be a wife, a Mom of three kids under the age of 3, minister the gospel of Christ, and yet remain sane while keeping my momentum, is by stealing away and getting alone with the Lord. In my home, naptime is our time!

Friend, hunger for the presence of the Lord, and make it a priority to turn off the cell phone, computer, TV, music, all noise and all distractions to talk with Father God. Most importantly, listen for Him to speak to you.

Get fired-up by His life-giving words.

Jesus Our Lord demonstrated this for us. He would steal away from the crowds who were following Him, and even from His disciples who were closest to Him, to pray and talk to Father God. Take some time to read Matthew 14. In this chapter there are a lot of things going on. In the midst of the great miracle of feeding the 5000 with the 5 loaves of bread and 2 fish, Peter walking on water, and the terrible news of John the Baptist being murdered, Jesus took several *stops* to be alone (vs. 13 & 22). When things are up AND when things look down, we are in need of quiet time with the Lord.

His Word is life! His Word is pure. His Word is strength. His Word is ALL things! Wisdom. Understanding. Health. Are you down and depressed? The Word will replace anti-depressants and give you peace beyond what you could imagine. I am living proof of reading Psalms over and over until His peace would overtake me and joy would fill my heart.

His Word gives direction. It is a lamp to your feet and a light for your path (Ps. 119:105), and will lead you down God's perfect plan for your life. How awesome is that?! His Word is perfect. Sister, I am sold on His Word. The Lord says, "I watch over my Word to perform it." (Jer. 1:12) Open up His Word and you will see that in Christ you have been blessed with EVERY spiritual blessing (Eph. 1:3). The Bible is filled with promises that are for you today, and Jesus declares He will fulfill them in your life. Goodness gracious! Falling in love with the Lord and His Word has been the BEST thing I could ever do for my spiritual journey and destiny! Give me a Bible and quiet time, and let me be for as long as I like, and it just might be for hours. Now that I'm married with children, I don't have as much free time as I did when I was single. So, single sister, take advantage of this awesome season in your life to grow in the Word and spend time with the Lord.

Feasting on His Word is like eating healthy food. Though we might not desire it up front, the more we eat healthy and drink our water, the more our body desires it. The more you read your Bible, the more you will want to. Ask the Lord to give you a burning passion for getting alone with Him in His Word.

Satan does NOT want you to have the Word in your heart. He will do everything to distract you from reading and desiring it. You can find a translation that you understand (I love the NKJV or NIV). Keep giving the Word a try. Read and meditate on scriptures. Choose a scripture that speaks to your heart and read it over and over again. Pull up www.blueletter.com and type in a bible verse to read it in different translations. Memorize verses and speak them out loud during the day. You can begin with one of my favorites, Joshua 1:8.

"Do not let this Book of the Law depart from your mouth; meditate on it day and night, so that you may be careful to do everything written in it. Then you will be prosperous and successful."

Wow! The Book of God's Holy Word will cause you to be successful when you read, meditate in it, and apply it.

I am still the girl who loves to get out, have fun, explore, and GO. I am also the girl who embraces, waits and daily pulls over to stop, rest, and re-fuel in the presence of the Lord. His Word keeps me nourished and energized. My stops with the Lord have made this the journey-of-a-lifetime!

Don't you SO love your passenger, Jesus Christ? I do. Maybe it's time to pull over, STOP, and love on Him for a moment. Once you're satisfied, turn the ignition. Rev-up Jetta. And GO! I'll see you on the freeway, girlfriend.

~*~

About the Author:
Deanna Bridges is a Super-Mom, empowered by Christ to fulfill her calling. This North Carolina native is an example of true beauty, everywhere she goes!
As our first ever *Crown of Beauty* cover-girl, we were so excited to have her face on the front of *The Beauty Issue.*
Deanna has a fiery passion for ministering to young women, and would love to come minister at your church. Check out her Facebook page! www.facebook.com/deannabridgesministries

Adventures in Africa

Imagine sitting in a group of five to fifteen orphans from a third-world country, and they were all asking you questions. What kind of questions would you expect?

The children and I usually sit in a tight circle, until it just becomes a tight knot with all of them leaning over in my lap and braiding my hair. This is when the questions are brought up. Many of the questions are the usual ones you ask when you first try to get to know someone. "How old are you?" Or, "What is your favorite food?" And even, "What grade are you in?" But these kids also wonder about things you wouldn't expect. One of the funniest conversations I have had with them concerns my retainers. (I got my braces off shortly before coming here, so I still have to wear my retainers all the time.)

One of my buddies named Elizabeth, age 12, had her head in my lap. As I was talking with one of the others, she jumped up and opened her eyes wide.

"What is that in your mouth?" She questioned.

I didn't know how to explain what they were, so I just stuck with, "My teeth were messed up so the dentist had to put them in my mouth to fix it."

She looked confused, and told all of the others they had to come and see the "things in her mouth."

Then the questions started rolling. "Is it glass?" "What do you do with them when you need to eat?" "Do all of your teeth come out with them?"

I explained again, and they seemed to partially understand.

Then finally the big question came. "Can you take them out and show us?"

I said no at first, but they were truly very curious and kept asking. So…I popped my top retainer off. I guess it must have scared them…because they all screamed!

They sat still for a moment after I put it back in, and then Elizabeth quietly said, "Do it again?"

There and Back Again

Who are missionaries? They are those partially crazy, super-Christians who sell all of their earthly possessions and move to third-world countries to help the poor, right?

That might not be the typical "Sunday School" answer, but nonetheless, that is what most of us think of the people with the label of "Missionary."

I was no exception. I had seen the strange people with radical faith come visit my church, talk about life in the mission field, share heart-wrenching pictures, and tell amazing stories. I looked at them like they were some sort of eccentric celebrities, following God to the ends of the earth, because HE told them to…How crazy is that? God, the Creator of the Universe, told them to do something outside the normal with their lives! He told them not to live the average, first-world-Christian lifestyle.

They always quoted Matthew 28:19 in all of their sharing sessions. I heard what it said, but I didn't really listen. "God won't call me to sell everything and move to a foreign country. I'm a fairly normal person. I'm not an ultra-mega-Christian. I'm just a kid in youth group, attending a medium-sized congregation, primarily concerned with good grades and hanging out with my friends. I'm not missionary material…"

I didn't really want to be. I was content to do a bit of ministry now and then, just enough to "get by," and sit in the pew every Sunday and Wednesday.

My world was turned upside down when my family was called to Kenya, Africa. How dare God, the God who created me and knows everything about me, decide to make plans that differed from mine!

I was angry; angry at my Maker for telling me something I didn't want to hear. I had friends, family, a church, a home, an entire life right where I was. Did He not care about any of that? I want to laugh and cry at the same time as I remember my thoughts and behavior at that time, at how wrong I was…Because God never stopped having my best interest in mind. He never asked anything more than to love Him and trust Him. And I always thought I was strong in my faith.

I was granted the opportunity to go on a short, ten-day trip a few months before we were scheduled to move. My perspective was completely changed. I realized that there are other people in this world. People who have so much faith in Christ, that mine seemed like a joke. People who were so joyful when they had nothing, I began to see just how much I take for granted. People who have such love with no prejudices. I felt right at home in a puddle of sewage. I fell in love with these people. I went there to teach them and help them, but they ended up teaching me! And it was amazing!

My dad, mom, four brothers, three sisters, and I moved in late September of 2013, a few days before I turned sixteen. I was ready and excited for the new adventure God had in store. Our main mission was to start and run a Guest House for incoming mission teams, train orphans from a local Children's Home to begin running it, and hope that the money gained from the house would help support the Children's Home.

Both working in the Guest-House and at the Children's Home rendered new relationships, great stories, and amazing opportunities to minister. My already-large family grew during that time, as did my heart.

"Why don't I love like that on a regular basis?"

Nothing can describe the feeling I got when a child from the Home, after braiding my hair, laid her head in my lap, looked up with her big brown eyes and said, "I wish you were my mother."

That is true love. Love that cannot see the color of someone's skin. Love that does not care about the fact that you came from a different culture. Love that sees the heart, not just the shell that holds it. Love that Jesus had for me.

"Why do I look for fulfillment in sources other than Christ?"

I was in awe when I saw pastors who traveled on foot for hours, just to make it to a weekly pastor's conference. They were so hungry for the Word, so completely fine with walking through rain and mud, to only hear It spoken for a few hours. These people with nothing were the ones who saw the truest treasure in the world.

As these questions and others accumulated, I slowly but surely slipped into a trap that many missionaries fall into...feeling judgmental.

I would see a random rant on the internet that ended with the common hashtag: "#firstworldprobs" and I would feel anger boil up inside. "You have no idea. do you?" I would think, harshly, "There are people in the world who would give anything to have a lifetime of your worst days..."

Little did I realize, I was forgetting to read my Bible for comfort and guidance. I was relying on my feelings to dictate my behavior. This crazed whirlwind of emotion began to affect my outlook on life, and my relationship with my family. Once I turned back to God's Word, things began to improve. I worked on mending my relationships with my dearest loved ones, and I began to feel better.

By the time February of 2014 rolled around, our mission had been completed. We had accomplished everything we knew God had sent us for, and then some!! Sometimes His timing is really crazy, because we had calculated for the mission to take two or three years; and it only took six months. We knew our time there was done, and it was time to come home.

Goodbyes were difficult. The children who I had become closest to, felt like family to me. I wanted to pack all of them into my suitcase and bring them back to America with me. And so did they.

In parting, I did my best to smile and keep my voice steady. But tears are difficult to hold back; especially when they are because of love. When we came home, we had no vehicle, no food, no furniture, and no house to put it all in. But we had people who loved us, and that's all that mattered.

Our church family generously provided a house, a vehicle, food,

furniture, and literally everything all the way down to the silverware in our kitchen drawer. As I write, I feel tears stinging my eyes because the beauty of love never ceases to amaze my heart.
So where am I now?

I am sitting in our house, and everything in my sight is a gift, given in love. I am a Senior in high school with my wonderful parents as my teachers. My dad is working at a cell phone company, and is looking for a church to pastor. My mother, as I said before, is working as one of the most amazing role models I could ever have. We all go to church every Sunday and Wednesday. I hang out with my friends and youth group all the time. I work with the nursery and kids' ministry every few weeks. Things are by all accounts "normal."

But normal is a funny word. I am living in practically the same life I was before. But there is something slightly different in the air…And it's not because that much changed back in the States while I was gone.

The change is internal, spiritual, and emotional. My perspective is different than it was before. I see things in a new way. Everything has a different meaning. I'm still not a super-Christian; I'm just a human. I have flaws, sins, and strong opinions. I can be stubborn when God tells me to follow His plan. I can still be quick to judge people who don't understand what I do. I didn't choose this plan for my life; God did. It isn't what I did; it was what God did with me. I am not the special one; God is.

I am being 100% honest when I say, "GOD'S PLAN IS BEST."
It worked out for me.
It will work out for you.
Live it out.

~*~

About the Author:
Hannah is a 18-year-old sister to seven, hailing from the friendly state of Texas. She passionately loves writing and can usually be found curled up with a book and a cup of iced coffee, or strumming her guitar on the back porch swing.

Check out Hannah's Blog: wilsonsisterto7.blogspot.com

Believe It

If you're anything like me, I'm sure you've thought out which style of wedding dress would complement your body shape best, and you've imagined your groom's face the first moment he sees you in it. You know exactly how many kids you want, and you've even determined you are going to name your oldest son after his father, Harry. You've probably imagined all the adventures you and your potential other will experience together, like skydiving or backpacking through Europe, maybe even swimming with dolphins. Well, some people might call you hopeless and obsessive, but I'd call you a dreamer.

A few years back, I was in a nearly three-year-long relationship with this boy (let's call him Bob) who I had fallen quite hard for. Together, we planned out our futures. Most of my thoughts were focused on Bob and planning out my life around him and with him. Being a dreamer, as I've previously mentioned, was mind- and time-consuming enough, but being a dreamer in love...I was a mess. I invested so much of my time, my heart, and my expectations into these dreams we built together; so much so, that when Bob (shockingly and suddenly, to me) up and left, my dreams were abolished. I had no future plans or ambitions that he wasn't a part of. (Pathetic, I know.)

It wasn't until months later when I found myself face down on my bedroom floor, weeping and questioning God why He would allow me to experience such loss, that He spoke to me. He reminded me that I was His daughter before anything else. He wanted my heart and my dreams before anyone. He showed me how much He wanted me to be invested in Him. Many times in His word it says that He is a "jealous God." He showed me just how much I had put Bob before Him. I was ashamed and embarrassed.

God had so many beautiful dreams planned for Him and me together, but I had chosen Bob and the dreams I built with him. With Bob, I felt like I had more control over my dreams. It was difficult for me to put my hopes and dreams in God's hands, knowing He would be the orchestrator of my dreams and not me.

I was trying to create new dreams on my own without God or Bob in mind, but nothing felt right. I felt empty and without clear direction. After months of struggling back and forth with God and myself, I finally gave in to God.

Thankfully, The Lord had already begun orchestrating my dreams without my knowledge. He opened up doors that I feared to open. But all the while, He kept whispering in my ear, "Don't worry! I've got you. Just take that first step of faith, and I promise I won't let you down." He wanted me to let go of things I held on to most, because they made me feel secure and in control. He again whispered, "Let me be your security. Put your trust in ME." So I did.

Here I am a completely different person because of that decision. I have new dreams, new ambition, and a new hope, all in The Lord. A song called "Pure and Holy Passion" describes my "dreamer's transformation," if you will. The chorus writes: "Give me one pure and holy passion. Give me one magnificent obsession. Give me one glorious ambition for my life: to KNOW and FOLLOW hard after YOU." Truly, I can say this is what The Lord gave me.

I have dreams that I never thought I'd be courageous enough to have. I am filled with peace that my dreams are the dreams He placed in me. Because of that, I know he will allow me to fulfill them for His glory. He says in Luke 1:45, "Blessed is she who believed." So, believe it.

I went from being a girl who had all her dreams invested in a boy; to being broken, shattered and hopeless without dreams; to now being a confident young woman whose dreams are fully invested in Jesus Christ, with the complete assurance of his plans for my life. Surely His plans and dreams for me are greater than any dreams I could have come up with on my own. I wouldn't trade His plans for me, for the world.

I encourage you that if you are a dreamer, let God do the dreaming for you. Invest your dreams in Jesus. You will be amazed by the life-changing adventures he plants in your heart. It might be scary to give Him reign over your dreams, but I promise you, you will not regret it.

~*~

About the Author:
Melody is a fun-loving dreamer from California. As a representative for Becoming Esther Ministries, she dreams of traveling the world and telling everyone about the love of Jesus.

Hollywood-Spun Dreams vs. Adventures with Jesus

Sweet harmonies float through my headphones and carry me across the turquoise ocean. When I open my eyes, I find myself standing on congested streets in London, where the pavement shines from rainfall. This music has led me to a magical lamp-post where I stumble backwards into a world that feels like Narnia. And here, I am lost for hours.

Time stands still. In this imaginary world, I feel like some kind of a Queen or a Duchess. I feel adored and admired. It's like I've been transported to Never, Never Land with a gang of lost boys who don't want to grow up. Here, they gently sit me down on a rock and serenade me with music, as if I am a gorgeous, red-headed mermaid in Mermaid Lagoon. Their lyrics are like healing balm on open sores that have been bleeding. The songs make me smile.

Here I am told that I am beautiful…that I am worth something…and that I am loved. No young guy in the real world has ever expressed these things to my jittery heart, and so coming to this dream place, I cling to my ticket of transportation known as my *One Direction* CD. I collect all the roses of adoration that *One Direction* tosses to me, and bow like the grateful princess that I am.

It is here that I am greeted with a reckless kind of love. A love that almost fools me into believing that it could be real. That I, along with ten-trillion other girls in the world, might actually have a chance at finding romance and life-long happiness with one of the *One Direction* guys.

Okay, stop laughing! If we we're being honest with each other, every teen girl has a goofy little fantasy hidden somewhere deep within her heart. We all have a secret route of escape to a world of unspoken, fairytale dreams. Whether you dream of slipping into the world of *Doctor Who*, running around with Peeta in the *Hunger Games*, or living in a tale by Jane Austen where you could dance with your very own Mr. Darcy...we are all guilty of attempting to escape reality.

Movies, novels, and our favorite songs have the power to lead our imaginations into some interesting places. In fact, most of us would admit that many of our "teenage dreams" were suggested by something we saw on television or read in a book. These "dreams" typically have to do with going on a grand adventure, falling in love, and being adored for who we really are. Let's call these, for lack of a better word, "Hollywood-Spun Dreams."

For example, my dream of running around London with the *One Direction* boys is a Hollywood-Spun dream. That wasn't something I was born with. I didn't reach five-years-old and think, "Wow, I really want to go to London and meet a cute boy."

But, long before I was in my mother's womb, God placed inside me the intrinsic desire for adventure and romance. The Lord put such a deep longing for these things (attention, affirmation, the desire to love and be loved), that when I saw my first Mary-Kate and Ashley teeny-bopper movie, something was awakened inside my heart...the dream of finding true love.

I thought that perhaps, like the movies projected, I could find true love in a boy with a great head of hair and a killer singing voice. What I didn't know was that these dreams couldn't be fulfilled in romance novels, or by listening to my favorite love songs. This dream craved something so much deeper.

Sister, we all have a ravenous hunger, something like an endless vacuum that cries out for God. Our hunger is a beautiful thing. It's what prompts us to seek God, search out purpose, and find Someone who will satisfy this desire. The only problem with having such a wild appetite is the danger of filling ourselves with the wrong things.

I am twenty-years-old and have never been on a date. There are days when I doubt someone will come along and make these "Hollywood-Spun" dreams come true. What we fail to sometimes realize is that these Hollywood-spun dreams are merely a shadow...a deceptive mirage of what we're truly seeking for. These Hollywood-spun dreams all-at-once dissolve into thin air when we stand in the Glory of His Royal Majesty. When we stare into the eyes of our Heavenly King, any and all earthly men pale in comparison. When our hearts are lifted to the heights of Heaven, and we explore the courts of our King's heart, we encounter the vision of beauty and pure love that we've always ached to find. It is in Him that we find our True Dream. Jesus is the epitome of everything our hearts could possibly long for.

"One thing I ask from the LORD, this only do I seek: that I may dwell in the house of the LORD all the days of my life, to gaze on the beauty of the LORD and to seek him in his temple." [Psalm 24:7]

"His mouth is sweetness itself; He is altogether lovely. This is my lover, this my friend, O daughters of Jerusalem."
[Song of Solomon 5:16]

"You are fairer [more handsome, more beautiful] than the sons of men; Grace is poured upon Your lips; Therefore God has blessed You forever." [Psalm 45:2]

Wrapped up inside the person of Jesus Christ is everything, and I mean everything we could ever dream. He puts all Disney Princes or funky-haired band members to shame. There is no man, friendship, experience, earthly adventure or pleasure that compares to Him. Jesus is our every dream come true.

"Well that's depressing," you might say. "I've been seeking God my whole life, and I know He is supposed to fill me up, I mean to a certain degree, but I still have such deep desires that are waiting to be fulfilled! Does this mean I can't daydream about going to London, feeding the hungry, getting married, or recording my own album?"

I'm not sure why, but for some reason, when we hear the truth that Jesus is everything we need, we begin to get scared. It causes a knee-jerk reaction as we reach for all our little dreams that have been scattered on the floor like tinker-toys. We hold these visions close to our heart and pray that God won't take them away from us. For some reason, we imagine that if Jesus is everything we need and desire...then our dreams will never come to pass.

This couldn't be further from the truth. In fact, the desires that are in you (not the Hollywood-spun ones, but the natural, purest form of who you are and what you long for as a person) have been designed by the King of Kings. Being totally fulfilled and satisfied in Him doesn't mean that all your dreams have to be thrown in the fire of sacrifice. Instead, God gave you these dreams so He could ENJOY THEM WITH YOU. He wants to be smack dab in the center of the day you say, "I do," fly to Africa the first time, or publish your novel. He knows that apart from Him, all these "dreams" are utterly meaningless. We've all seen Bridezilla stress over her special day, celebrities who complain about life in the spotlight, burned out preachers, and frazzled moms who just wish they were single again. I've often looked at people who are living my "dream" life, and think, "How can you possibly complain about anything!? You're the luckiest girl ever!"

But without Jesus, any of these dreams can turn into terrible burdens. Without the supernatural joy and peace of walking side-by-side with our Savior, chasing dreams can suddenly turn into chasing a cold, harsh wind. It's all dead and pointless.

So, even though our souls are to be 100% satisfied in Jesus, we cannot remain where we are at spiritually, in our relationships, and in the pursuit of our dreams. It's time we get excited about our future and start running!

God loves to play Hide-and-Go-Seek. There's a reason that He loves for us to seek Him. He loves the romance and adventure of bounding ahead of us on this trail, then calling our name, "Come after me, come after me! Come hear what I have to say to you! You're going to LOVE what's around this next corner!"

He could, if He wanted to, make things ridiculously easy for us by holding our hand every second along this trail, explaining not to be afraid if a snake pops out of the bushes, or what to do if the hill gets steep...but He knows that if He did that, we would never grow. He wants our hearts to grow in courage and strength! He wants us to climb mountains of seemingly impossible situations, and run after Him like our lives depend on it! When we experience dissatisfaction with who we are or what our lives look like, that's His gentle way of nudging us to take a few more steps forward, peek around the trees, call out for His name, and see if we can find Him. In the same way, our dreams have been placed inside of us so that we take action, and go after them with Jesus.

There are certain aspects of the character of Christ that we will never know or experience until we live it out with Him. The Word of God is meant to be EXPERIENCED and lived out loud. We can't just read about Peter walking on water or Esther coming before the king on behalf of her people. If we want to know God, we have to walk with God, and that means doing everyday life with Him.

Yes, we can absolutely get to know Jesus through prayer, reading the Word, and worship, but there comes a time in your life when the appetite for adventure and knowing God flings you out into the beautiful place of PURSUING A DREAM with Jesus.

If we long to know Jesus in this way, on such a real, tangible level, we have to MOVE. Every adventure begins by taking a first step.

If you're not sure what you want to do with your life, just pick a problem (this world is full of 'em). Then, choose something that you absolutely

LOVE to do. It can be singing, scrapbooking, web designing, teaching, math, interior design, or anything else! Think back to life as a little girl, and ask yourself, "What did I have a blast doing? What activity do I enjoy today? What gets my heart beating faster than anything? When do I feel totally alive?" Write down your answer. You might have one answer, or you may have ten! It's okay, when I did this at age fourteen, I had about thirty answers.

Now, put those two together (the problem you want to see solved in this world, and the one thing you absolutely LOVE doing), and use the latter to serve the former. Do you love scrapbooking? Does human trafficking rip your heart apart? Why not design scrapbook pages, sell them on Etsy, and donate all the money to an anti-trafficking organization? What about party planning? Use your love for parties to offer a free kids' party service for single moms who are struggling and stressed. These are just examples, but are you getting the idea?

So often we, as Christian girls, sit around and wait for God to "show us what we're supposed to do with our lives," and all the while hungry children are starving, and kids at school are committing suicide. I know that it feels like the "spiritual" thing to do...to wait until we are absolutely positive that it's the Lord's direction before starting a project. But do we really think the Lord will freak out if we "accidently" do good and help make someone's life AMAZING, even if it's not in His "perfect plan" for our lives? That sounds so silly when we say it out loud!

Sister, if your heart is stirred by a problem in this world, don't sit around and wait for a prophet to show up on your door step and say, "Thus saith the Lord!"

We already know His commands to love our neighbors, go make disciples, love the unlovable, set the captives free, speak up for the rights of the destitute, make unjust and crooked paths straight, and be the salt and light of the world. So what are we waiting for?

Sometimes I think the Lord is just waiting for us to CHOOSE something, and go do it with Him!

The imaginary games we played as children, and things we imagined and desired were like road maps for our future. God has placed burning visions inside each of us, desires we had long before Hollywood came along and suggested we be "pretty, famous, and popular."

When we daydream about the impact we could have if we put others before ourselves, and the gifts we could use for God's glory, we realize that our inner blueprint of desire is actually a SOLUTION for this world. You were all created to be an ANSWER.

I've heard it said that faith is stepping out before the staircase arrives. Faith is not sitting around thinking, "Well, I'm just gonna have fun and be a teenager, until I grow up and find what God wants me to do."

I'm going to use my story for example, not because I think it's so spectacular or am trying to puff myself up, but I want you to see what God can do when you simply GIVE Him something to work with.

The problem I chose to confront was distorted self-image. My heart was ripped apart by the tragedy that girls struggle with eating disorders, compare themselves with Hollywood, hate themselves, and are deceived about who they really are. And so, after choosing a problem which I believed the Lord could use me to make a massive dent in, I chose a method of solution. I picked something I absolutely LOVED, which were magazines. I had a strange obsession over them as a child, and it only made sense that I could design and create my own.

I didn't hear the Lord say, "Thou shalt start *Crown of Beauty Magazine!*" In fact, I wasn't even sure if that was the exact direction He wanted me to go. I could have chosen many other paths. I could have chosen to pursue singing and the music industry, acting and being a light in Hollywood, or writing my own books and trying to get them published.

But I picked something that I knew I would have fun with. I wasn't even sure how long I would do it for, or if it would reach very many people, but I picked SOMETHING while I was waiting for God to open other doors that were still closed to me.

The Lord has blessed this magazine, and used it to touch hearts, simply because I GAVE Jesus something to work with. Just like the little boy who offered Jesus the fishes and loaves. When we give Him our lives, He can bless us, break us, and then give us away. It's our prayer that this issue may be the launching pad that shoots you on a grand adventure with Christ...abandoning your "Hollywood-spun" dreams, for the one TRUE Dream: You and Jesus, changing the world together.

~*~

Simply Be

When we think of missions we usually think of Africa, starving children and cannibal tribes chasing us across the river as we try to preach the Gospel to them. Well, at least that is what I used to think when I heard the word "missions." I never saw myself as a "missionary." Then God spoke the word "nations" to me repetitively for a series of months, about two years ago. I was trying to figure out what my major was going to be when I went college. It is a ministry college, and I only had a few options. I could have chosen any one of them because I had a passion for almost all of them. The last major I saw myself doing was "Missions." I did not feel called to living in a foreign country and learning different languages. My heart did want to travel, but I did not see myself as the typical missionary type.

Over those couple of months I kept hearing and seeing the word "nations" everywhere. This prompted me to seek and pray even more. So I began to pray and seek out what Abba Father was trying to tell me. I began to do research on what a missionary actually does and where the word came from. When I looked up the definition of a missionary on Wikipedia.com it stated that, "A missionary is a member of a religious group sent into an area to do evangelism or ministries of service, such as education, literacy, social justice, health care and economic development. The word 'mission' originates from 1598 when the Jesuits sent members abroad, derived from the Latin 'missionem' (nom. missio), meaning 'act of sending' or 'mittere', meaning 'to send'. The word was used in light of its biblical usage; in the Latin translation of the Bible, Christ uses the word when sending the disciples to preach in his name."

I was ecstatic when I read this. I always said I wanted to be able to do many different things in life. I desired to have many different life skills so I could do just about anything. My heart did not know that it was made to be a missionary. Missionaries are the preachers, the teachers, the lawyers, the doctors and more. They come to a place and make it better.

The lives of the people encountered by a missionary are forever transformed. Missionaries are people that see a need and find a solution. Missionaries are passionate about the places God puts them. Missionaries leave people, conversations, homes, and nations better off than when they came. They are world changers; they are home changers.

God has placed you somewhere, in some town, in some work environment and in some family. You have a mission. The King has sent you as an Ambassador for Christ into some environment to be who you are as a daughter of God. Who you are as a daughter of God and co-heir with Christ is the most powerful thing that you have. When you walk into a room, you carry Jesus; you carry His heart. Whether people know this or not is up to you. As a daughter of the King, you carry the Kingdom of Light into every dominion of darkness by simply being your true self. Your true self is the identity that Jesus gave you when you gave your life to Him and chose to walk with Him.

He calls you His Bride. He calls you Anointed. He calls you Chosen. He calls you Pure. He calls you Lovely. He calls you Righteous. These are the names HE has given you. When you walk as a daughter of Light into dark places, you are being a missionary.

In this season, I am learning to be faithful where God has placed me. I am a second-year college student with a very busy life. Working, going to class, being on a dance team, and being a part of school outreaches, can seem like too much when I am not looking to Jesus. It becomes very hard when I do not set my mind on things above (Colossians 3). I have become overwhelmed at times with everything and even frustrated, but Abba Father gave me a choice. He told me to quit trying so hard and simply be His daughter. That meant imitating His Son Jesus! My choice is to either imitate Christ, who for the JOY that was set before Him endured the cross, or give up because the mission seems too hard (Hebrews 12). I refuse to give up. Hard is not in my vocabulary. I choose joy.

I am in training right now; the mission God has given me is to simply be His daughter, a student of His Word and to love my peers, coworkers, leaders and all I come in contact with. My life is my mission field, and I will win the race set before me. Be bright with the light of the Gospel shining through your face. Be kind in the words you speak to people. Be generous with love, money and time. Be understanding when people sin against you and hurt you. Be forgiving to them. Be pure in heart by checking your motives and repenting of hidden sins. Be obedient to a Father that you can trust. Be bold because the righteous are as bold as a lion. Be brave in the face of the impossible. Be honorable to those over you, even when you do not agree. Be LOVE to all.

He has equipped you. Your mission is to be His daughter and to love His Son with all your heart, soul, mind and strength. Your mission is to be His girl and nothing more. He will show you what you must do. Be brave Beautiful, for He is with you!

Captivated by His Love,
Nellie Martin

~*~

QUIZ! What Kind of Mission Field
Were You Made For?

Not sure where God wants your mission field to be?

"And He gave some as apostles, and some as prophets, and some as evangelists, and some as pastors and teachers, for the equipping of the saints for the work of service, to the building up of the body of Christ..." {Ephesians 4:11}

There is no "one-size-fits-all" for a missionary. In Christ, we are all called to change this world. Take our quiz to discover where your unique mission field might be!

1. It's Saturday! How are you going to spend your sweet hours of free time?

A. Babysitting. I will either be occupied watching my little siblings, my pastor's kids, or another child from the neighborhood. Someone is always calling me to be Super Nanny!

B. Daydreaming. I might sketch out fresh ideas for a movie script, write a new song, Pin some inspirational quotes, or choreograph a new dance. You never know what new idea will pop into my mind!

C. Working. I get a strange sort of satisfaction from working hard, and bringing home a paycheck.

D. Making a new beauty video for YouTube! If not that, you can find me watching my favorite Beauty Guru's, shopping at the mall, sorting through my accessories, or designing new outfits in my sketch book.

E. Hanging out with my best friends, planning something fun like a sleepover party, game night, or surprise party for a friend at church.

F. I lock myself in my bedroom and write!

G. Doing whatever needs to get done. The dishes, laundry, catching up on emails, or texting my friends.

H. I Google "Youth Mission Trips" online, and read about trips that I long to take.

I. My day is spent worshiping the Lord. I maybe write some new songs, and just spend time singing for my King.

2. Your best friend just had the worst day of her life. Your heart is breaking for her, and you want to do something to show her you care. What do you do?

A. I offer to help her out with responsibilities at home. I watch her little siblings for an evening, so she can spend some much needed alone time.

B. I treat her to a movie and some ice cream. If I can't afford that, we will just hang out in my bedroom, singing karaoke all night long, until we're laughing so hard that she forgets about all her worries.

C. I reschedule all my other activities so we can spend time talking. I will always be her shoulder to cry on.

D. I take her to the mall, buy her a new outfit, and then give her a fabulous makeover back at the house!

E. I share some of my favorite scripture verses, in hopes to encourage her.

F. I write her a long, six-page letter, just to let her know how much I love her.

G. I race over to her house, and be whatever she needs me to be! Whether she needs a shoulder to cry on, a friend to laugh with, or some encouragement: I want to be all of that.

H. I remind her of the future, and all our fabulous plans. She can't help but smile when I remind her of all our future "someday" trips!

I. We worship together. Getting into God's presence is the quickest way to let every care melt away in His love!

3. Don't look now! But the guy you've had a crush on for three years is looking your way! You're super excited, because he is your absolute dream dude! What is his personality like?

A. He loves kids. Nothing makes me melt more than to see him running around with the kiddos at church, playing tag and pretending to get caught, even though he could totally outrun them if he tried! He is going to make such an amazing daddy some day!

B. Welllll....he plays guitar. And sings. He's a great people person, and has a desire to direct Christian movies someday. What a holy hunk!

C. He has a great head on his shoulders, and is very successful in his field of business. He is so driven and motivated, it's inspiring. He will be a great provider for some lucky girl!

D. He is an absolute sweetheart. He doesn't think I'm strange...he actually understands me! Plus, he went to the mall as I shopped for hours, without once complaining. He is a keeper!

E. He is a naturally-born leader. He has a passion to minister to teens, and is planning on becoming a Youth Pastor someday. Umm...I wouldn't totally object to being a youth pastor's wife.

F. He is spunky, spontaneous, and wants to travel the world! Isn't that what every girl wants? To travel the world with the man she loves? I can totally see myself blogging about all this.

G. He has the heart of a servant, through and through. He isn't overly outgoing, but rather soft and steady. I believe that he would be my biggest supporter and cheerleader, and for that...I love him!

H. He desires to be a missionary in a foreign land. His heart is the most handsome and attractive thing I have ever seen! Is it too much to want to be his wife?

I. He has a passionate heart for worship. He doesn't just lead worship on the platform...but he leads worship with his life. I would be more than happy to submit my heart to him, and follow his lead!

4. Congrats! You just landed your dream job! What are you doing?

A. Working with kids. Maybe I am an elementary or preschool teacher. Or perhaps I am homeschooling my own kids at home! Whatever it is, you can bet it involves kids.

B. I'm doing something in the entertainment industry. Whether I am directing films, writing TV scripts, or starring in them...you can be sure I am in my sweet spot! Maybe I'm recording an album, or going on tour.

C. I'm not totally sure. (That's why I'm taking this quiz!) But probably in a successful, well-paid profession, such as nursing, dentistry, sales and marketing, or anything in the professional business industry.

D. I'm involved with the beauty and fashion industry! I might be a cosmetologist, makeup artist, fashion designer, stylist, or work for a beauty and fashion magazine.

E. Working with youth. I may be a counselor, work at a summer camp, or get involved with a full time youth ministry. Whatever it is, I just want to pour into young adults. I might even be a youth pastor!

F. I'm writing, traveling, blogging, traveling, and writing some more. I could be a published author, a magazine columnist, a pro-blogger, or full-time travel agent!

G. I have no idea. (Or maybe I do know, but it wasn't listed as an option for this question...) but I just want to be serving and loving the people around me, washing their feet like Jesus would, being their biggest supporter and cheerleader!

H. I am serving in a foreign country. It breaks my heart to see so much pain and suffering. I believe God is going to send me out as a missionary to foreign lands!

I. I am a worship leader at church, or perhaps I've recorded a worship album. Maybe I lead worship for a youth group, or just lead worship with my kids and dance around the living room for God's glory! Whatever it is, it has to do with music.

5. Oh no! Your house is on fire! Quick, you can only grab one item! What is it?

A. My family scrapbook/photo-album. Our memories are so important to me!

B. My iPod! I cannot survive without my music!

C. My purse/wallet. It has all my necessities.

D. My makeup, shoes, and clothes. I have some favorites that would be hard to replace!

E. My cell phone. Not being able to contact my friends would be absolute torture.

F. My favorite books. I can't bear to watch them burn!

G. Letters from my best friends. I can't lose those.

H. Nothing...I just want to get everyone out as fast as possible.

I. My guitar!

6. Which of the following Bible verses is your favorite?

A. "The King will reply, 'Truly I tell you, whatever you did for one of the least of these brothers and sisters of mine, you did for me.' " {Matthew 25:40}

B. "You are the light of the world. A town built on a hill cannot be hidden." {Matthew 5:14}

C. "Being confident of this, that he who began a good work in you will carry it on to completion until the day of Christ Jesus." {Philippians 1:6}

D. "I praise you because I am fearfully and wonderfully made; your works are wonderful, I know that full well." {Psalm 139:14}

E. "For I know the plans I have for you," declares the Lord, "plans to prosper you and not to harm you, plans to give you hope and a future." {Jeremiah 29:11}

F. "When I consider Your heavens, the work of Your fingers, the moon and the stars, which You have ordained; What is man that You take thought of him, and the son of man that You care for him?" {Psalm 8:3}

G. "But you, Lord, are a shield around me, my glory, the One who lifts my head high." {Psalm 3:3}

H. "For whoever wants to save their life will lose it, but whoever loses their life for Me will save it." {Luke 9:24}

I. "Let everything that has breath praise the Lord. Praise the Lord." {Psalm 150:6}

7. Which of these women do you feel like you relate with, and look up to the most?

A. Mrs. Duggar! It's a miracle that she can handle a household of nineteen kids with such ease. She reminds me so much of the Proverbs 31 woman.

B. Taylor Swift. I love that she has been in the music industry for so long, and still manages to be a fairly good role model for girls...especially considering our other options in Hollywood!

C. I admire any woman who pursues a professional career, is successful in her field, and can manage it all with a humble spirit.

D. Bethany Mota! I love her story. She is my favorite YouTuber. I hope to have my own fashion line, just like her someday!

E. My youth leader, Sunday school teacher, or another woman in our church who has impacted my life in an amazing way.

F. My favorite author! Every time I read her words, I am instantly drawn into the story. So inspiring!

G. My best friend. She encourages me so much, and always knows what to tell me when I'm having a terrible day.

H. Mother Teresa. What an amazing woman. I also love the stories of Gladys Aylward, Catherine Booth, Heidi Baker, and Katie Davis (author of *Kisses from Katie.*)

I. Kari Jobe! She has such an anointing for worship on her life. I admire her in so many ways.

8. Which of these quotes are totally you?

A. "The most precious jewels you'll ever have around your neck are the arms of children."

B. "You cannot change the world if you are just like it."

C. "Spend your life building your dream. Or else you will spend it building someone else's."

D. "Beauty begins the moment you decide to be yourself."

E. "Life shrinks or expands in proportion to one's courage."

F. "If you don't see the book on the shelf that you want to read, then write it."

G. "It's not about falling down....it's about getting back up."

H. "Travel as much as you can, as far as you can, for as long as you can. Life is not meant to be lived in one place."

I. "Worship is born in our hearts, not on our lips."

If you got mostly A's...
You have a passion for **working with kids.** There is such great honor and high reward for those in the Kingdom who humble themselves to love on, care for, and pour into our next generation of world changers. If children are your mission field, here are some ideas of things you can be doing RIGHT NOW!

Offer a free babysitting or after school care service for the kids in your neighborhood. Start an after school book club for girls ages 8 to 12. Host a princess party for your favorite little girl, invite all her friends, and teach them about what it means to be royalty. Dream up a theme, and start your own afternoon summer camp for the kids that you know. Pick up your favorite little kid and spend an afternoon of carefree timelessness with them, showing 'em just how much you care! Make homemade ice-cream, have an afternoon art session, or ask a homeschooling mom if you can help her teach classes for the day. The opportunities in the mission field of little kids are absolutely endless!

If you got mostly B's...
Chances are pretty good that you have a desire to be involved with **the entertainment industry**. Whether that means you want to be behind the camera, in front of it, on the radio, or playing in a band...you may be called to be a Hollywood Missionary. So what practical action steps can you take today, in order to see these dreams become a reality tomorrow?

Pray for other Christians in Hollywood. Intercede for Godly entertainment, and Christian role models to rise up. Start a Bible study with your friends and host your own prayer meeting to lift up celebrities. Start a YouTube channel, sharing the songs you've written. Start a blog. Begin gaining a following on social media accounts, and be a good steward of what you've been given. Submit videos for a Disney Channel audition. Start a Christian actors and songwriters club at your school or church. Write your dream scripts and gather up a group of friends to perform your plays. Film short videos. Launch a project on Kickstarter to raise money for your dream pilot episode or movie. Network and connect with other singers and song writers. Collaborate with your writing. Use your gifts as an afterschool outreach. Share your music with anyone who will listen. Just get out there, and invade Hollywood and the entertainment industry with the light of Jesus Christ!

If you got mostly C's..
You probably have a knack for **the business world**. If the idea of working in a board room, dentist office, being a lawyer or owning your own business is appealing to you...chances are pretty good that the workforce is YOUR mission field! There are lost and broken people all around you wherever you work. We need Christians in the business world! Don't feel ashamed about what God has called you to do or succumb to the lie that having a professional career is any less powerful than building homes in Africa. Now is the time for you to take action and press on toward the dream God has placed in your heart!

Learn as much as you possibly can about your trade. Read books, interview successful people, and ask tons of questions. Study from the most excellent in your field. Learn their secrets and trades and commit everything you do to Jesus Christ. Go to conferences. Listen to wise teachers. Keep a journal about everything that you're learning. Stay focused and steady and you will make an impact in the field God has called you to!

If you got mostly D's...
You are a little miss **fashion diva**! (But in the absolute best sense of the word ;). God has given you a desire to explore beauty and sparkly things...and some people might not understand that. But the truth is we need Godly people in the twisted and deceptive beauty and fashion industries. What steps can you begin taking to make a huge impact in the fashion and beauty mission field?

Have a firm foundation in the Word. Know what God says about true beauty, and that this temporary life is so fleeting. Resolve in your heart that your mission is to draw attention to the inward and eternal by using something that the world is so obsessed with. Keep a journal and make clear the vision. Doodle out your wildest dreams. Start a YouTube channel, and make your own fashion vids. Start a fashion blog, and keep your followers updated. Network with other like-minded people. Submit your work to online blogs and magazines. If you're interested in the magazine world, apply for an internship. Work at your favorite clothing store. Study your craft, and learn as much about it as you possibly can. Create your own designs, and work to make them a reality...one piece at a time. Google local fashion and modeling shows and find out how you can get involved. Attend events. Have a business card. Know what it is that you want to offer to this world and come up with a strategic plan to do so.

If you got mostly E's...
You have a heart for **working with youth**! There are so many ways you can fully engage in this mission field.

Volunteer or work at a summer camp. Ask your Youth Leaders at church what you can do to help out. Plan some big outreach events to connect with unsaved teens in your area. Start a Bible Study group. Intercede for your High School. Start a weekly prayer group that meets at your house. Start a Twitter account to spread the gospel. Dive into the Word, and ask the Lord for wisdom and advice to share with young people when they ask for it. Go the extra mile to connect with your friends. Text them frequently, and ask them what they need prayer for. Be an amazing, safe friend; who doesn't gossip, spill secrets, or talk badly about others. Plan a *Crown of Beauty Conference* in your area (Contact us, and we'd love to help you set that up!), or a *COB* Bible Study (we will provide the study materials!). Start a Youth Page on Facebook for prayer requests, praise reports, and daily encouragement. Simply engage whole-heartedly with the teens around you, and watch and see what God will do!

If you got mostly F's...
You probably have a passion for **beautiful words and beautiful places**! If you adore writing, allow God to use you in that mission field! There are so many things you can be doing with your gifts and talents right now.

Start a blog, write an e-book, or use a self-publishing company to release your first book! Build a faithful following of readers on social media platforms such as Twitter, Instagram, and Facebook, and once your project is released, you can go on a virtual "Book Tour" to promote it! Seek the Lord with your desire to use this gift, and He will be faithful to direct your path! (Proverbs 3:5-6.)

If you got mostly G's...
It sounds like you are an absolute **servant at heart**. Sometimes, you might feel confused at the lack of 'clear direction' in your life. You may see that as a problem...but the truth is God has designed you as a humble follower and hard worker for a reason! Trust me. The radical visionaries who are full of ideas NEED you! You are a huge answer to prayer for the people around you! You are quick to jump in and help without being asked...there is a huge blessing in store for you! You love being the hands and feet to other people's projects...and that is an amazing thing! Jesus said the greatest in the Kingdom of Heaven are the very least...those who humble themselves in order to make other people look amazing. You can have peace about where you are at...bloom where you are planted! Volunteer for new projects, serve wherever you can, and learn about as many things as possible!

If you got mostly H's...
You are a little **Miss Missionary**! It's undeniable. Your heart is in foreign lands. Girl, it's time to get your passport. Begin brainstorming ideas to raise money for your next mission trip. Pray and ask God to prepare you for the adventures and challenges ahead! Get connected with like-minded people who will be taking mission trips, and ask if you can tag along! You know where your heart lies...get out there and change the world! If you feel like you don't have any missionary connections, send us an email and we will see if we can hook you up. Enjoy flipping through this issue and meeting missionaries who started in the same place you did. All things are possible!

If you got mostly I's...
You are a **worship warrior**. Your role in the Kingdom is so vital. Atmospheres shift and strongholds break whenever YOU lift up a song of praise to the King. When you play guitar and write worship songs in

your room...you are in the heat of the mission field. God uses your praises like a weapon in His hand.

Sing the Psalms. Rewrite the Psalms and turn them into your own songs! Take some songwriting classes. Learn new instruments. Interview worship leaders and learn from them. Teach little kids about worship. Study the Word of God, and read every passage that has to do with having a heart of worship, and dive into what that looked like in the Old Testament vs. the New Testament. Mingle your worship time with your prayer time, by singing your prayers, and interceding for everyone you can think of. Spend as many hours as you possibly can in the presence of the King, pouring your love on Him, and you will without a doubt change this world!

~*~

7 Steps to Change the World

The greatest tragedy in life is not that men and women are being persecuted and killed for what they believe in; a far greater tragedy is that millions of people on this planet are living without any purpose or passion.

"What is the meaning of life?"

You can Google it or ask Siri, and you'll hear hundreds of answers. Siri once answered matter of factly, "All evidence to date suggests its chocolate." And while it's hard not to daydream about a world where chocolate is the purpose of our existence, in all seriousness we need to realize that most of the people we know are living without a purpose. Everyone dies, but not everyone lives. It is our job, as Christians, to strike a match in the dry places of their hearts and light them on fire for the King of Kings! Our passion is to pursue Jesus; living for Him is what should bring us to life! Quite often, however, we lose our spark, and the flame of passion dies inside of us. So many Christians have fallen prey to the lie that "life is all about me," and lead monotonous, boring, self-centered lives. If there is even an inch of complacency or questioning within your heart about why you're breathing, I want to challenge you with this article. Jesus paid much too high a price for us to be stuck in the rut of everyday life. Christianity without passion and freedom in Christ is just dead ole' religion. He died so that we might live, and live life to the fullest! What this world needs is to see you fully alive in Christ.

Jesus said, "Woe to you, teachers of the law and Pharisees, you hypocrites! You are like whitewashed tombs, which look beautiful on the outside, but on the inside are full of the bones of the dead and everything unclean." Matthew 23:27.

I don't want to have a dead heart like a stuffy, religious Pharisee. I want to be fully alive!

1. The Main Purpose of Your Life

Are you ready? It's simple, yet so excitingly exhilarating and profound! Matthew 22:37-38 says, "Love the Lord your God with all your heart, soul, mind and strength."

You were created to fall in love with Christ, know Him on a deep and intimate level and have a real relationship with the God who breathed out the stars! That is mind blowing! You were designed for Him. The affections of your heart long to be awakened to this truth. You were tailor-made to experience this love, to walk with and pour out your love upon Him. As He reveals His love to you and pours it into your heart, it is your honor and highest calling in life to pour it back onto Him! Like Mary in John 12:3, you get to break open the perfume of your life and pour it onto His feet.

2. It Doesn't End There

Jesus continues to explain the whole "changing of the world" part by adding, "Love your neighbor as yourself." There are many ways in which this love can be expressed, but it's important to realize that in order to love the people around us, we have to learn to love ourselves in a Christ-honoring way. If we hate and devalue ourselves, how are we going to learn to love and cherish one another? The only way we can truly love ourselves for Christ's sake, is by seeing ourselves through His eyes. We must focus on the high price He paid on the cross. The price that Jesus paid, loudly exclaims your worth to Him and the amazing worth of the people around you. You are His beloved inheritance and the prize of His heart! (See Ephesians 1:18.)

We have to value and honor the people around us, celebrating the fact that they are made in the image of God! Everyone is precious in the eyes of the King. Learn to see your friends, family and even absolute strangers as unique gifts from God. Learn to appreciate their diversity, special strengths and gifts.

"Therefore, as we have opportunity, let us do good to all people, especially to those who belong to the family of believers." Galatians 6:10

Let's treat our brothers and sisters with love, honoring them for who they truly are...kings and queens, sons and daughters of the King. How would you treat the Duchess of Cambridge, Princess Kate, if she came over to your house? You would honor her and treat her like royalty! Remember, "Whatever you do unto the least of my brothers, you do unto Me." Matthew 25:40

3. Changing the World Through Love

The world is really big. Trying to change it all at once is such a vast concept and a frightening task. So what are some practical things that will actually make a difference in the lives of those around you?

You could ask the waitress at your favorite restaurant if you can pray for her; offer to babysit your neighbor's kids for free; cook a meal for someone and drop it off at their house; write a letter of encouragement to the kid at your school who is always being bullied. Encourage everyone and speak life everywhere you go! Jesus said, "Go and make disciples of all nations, baptizing them in the name of the Father, Son and Holy Spirit." The word disciple means "learner." So lead and teach with your life. If you see a situation where someone is suffering, hurting, or is simply down in the dumps, get in there and do something about it! Jesus told us to "Heal the sick, raise the dead, cleanse those who have leprosy, cast out demons. Freely you have received. Freely give." Matthew 10:8. If you see a situation where Hell is getting the upper hand, go in and change it. Petition Heaven and make the wrongs right!

4. Bring Heaven to Earth

As an ambassador of Heaven you have been called to be a minister of peace and reconciliation! That means your job is to represent the heart of the King wherever you go! We can do that by praying and lifting our voice to the King, like Esther did. We can be confident in the fact that

God hears us! We also bring Heaven to Earth by caring about the things that He cares about and expressing that through our lives. When girls say, "I don't know what I'm supposed to do with my life," I always tell them, "Find an injustice (something that is wrong with the world) and bring God's heart into the situation. Go change it!"That's what you can do with your life; whether it's caring for orphans, setting people free from human trafficking, starting a Bible study group at school, teaching at a public school, restoring holiness in the arts and entertainment industry, or ministering to folks at a retirement home. The opportunities are endless! As His royal people, we were called for such a time as this. This is not the time to sit around and do nothing, but to get up and go!

5. Dream On
Live out your unique, God-given dreams! Just like in the "Parable of the Talents," you have been given a dream to steward. Your little dream is just a tiny sliver of God's massive dream for all History, His Story! He has been writing His Story across the canvas of history ever since the Garden of Eden. Your role on Earth is about so much more than yourself. The baton has been passed on to you and God wants to continue writing His Story! He wants to see His dream come to pass, and that requires you to follow the inner road map of desires and dreams in your heart! We have a great cloud of witnesses cheering us on, encouraging us to run the race set before us! Moses, Joseph, Esther; all of those folks were given a tiny sliver of God's big dream, and they were found faithful. Our lives are the same way. We only have an allotted number of days to do the things God has planted inside us, so GO FOR IT.

Don't wait for someone's permission to write your first book, build an orphanage or start your own business. It is vital that you live the unique role that God has set before you. Your dream doesn't look like my dream because your personality is totally different from mine. That's awesome! You might like numbers and I might like music, but we need both of our dreams to fulfill God's BIG dream.

6. Change the Culture

Daniel lived in a very crooked and perverse culture, just like we do. Daniel understood, however, the secret of Romans 12:2, even though he lived before that scripture was written and revealed to Paul! "Do not conform to the pattern of this world, but be transformed by the renewing of you mind. Then you will be able to test and approve God's will. His good, pleasing, and perfect will."

If we, like Daniel, can dive into the Word of God and allow our minds to daily be changed and transformed by Him, we won't live or think like this world. If we live in this counter-culture, according to the Kingdom of Heaven, we will shine like stars in the universe! (See Philippians 2:14-15) Living as daughters of the Most High sets us apart from the patterns and mind-sets of this world. Those around us might not always like what they see but when we light up, they will most certainly take note.

"In every matter of wisdom and understanding about which the king questioned them, he found them (Daniel and his friends) ten times better than all the magicians and enchanters in his whole kingdom." Daniel 1:20

One man's life can have an immeasurably huge impact! You are royalty; therefore you were predestined to have influence. I challenge you to step out into the world and live a radically different life. You never know who is watching you, following you and will choose to live like you. "Always be prepared to give an answer to everyone who asks you to give the reason for the hope that you have. But do this with gentleness and respect." 1 Peter 3:5

7. Change the World Through Your Family

Isn't it interesting that Jesus lived as a family man for 30 years of his life on Earth, before He started His "ministry"? We all desire to conquer the world and do great exploits for the Kingdom, but we have to realize that this journey of changing the world begins in our own homes! Many of us dream about someday becoming wives and mothers. There are days when all I want to do is give little kids baths, get them in their jammies, snuggle up, read to them and tuck them into bed! Having the desire to nurture and care for our someday families is totally natural. Being a mama is powerful! Not only are you affecting your kids, but you are changing lives for generations to come.

I believe one of the most powerful movements sweeping across the earth right now is a generation of young men and women who are saying "yes" to God, "yes" to purity and allowing God to write their love stories! When these beautiful marriages take place, it's a shining example of Jesus and His Bride! These couples are then blessed to raise households strong in the faith. Mothers are laying down their lives daily to pour into and teach their children the ways of the Kingdom. Children are our future world changers. If we can pour into them today, we are planting a seed of victory for tomorrow, the next day, and long after we're gone. That's what I call being eternally minded!

God's story is big and long, and so much greater than ourselves. Let's keep this perspective and be patient as we wait for His goodness to unfold in the lives of our future families.

~*~

Beyond the Veil of Deception

Have you ever wondered about other religions? Perhaps you've been raised in a Christian church your whole life, and you can't help but wonder what life would be like if we, as Christians, were wrong about what we believe.

Sometimes the enemy can plant pesky doubts in our minds. Doubts that whisper, "What if...What if there is no God? What if Jesus is just a fairytale? What about those other religions? What do they have to offer? What is the TRUTH?"

Meet Hannah T. She used to ask herself these same questions, and one day the doubt pushed her overboard. She jumped the ship of her Christian faith and found herself in the belly of a big black whale! Next thing she knew, Hannah was on her hands and knees, worshiping a false god, living life as a self-proclaimed Muslim. Check out her amazing story!

The Calm Before the Storm
Hannah grew up in a Christian church. She recalls memories of her childhood as a little girl; a happy, carefree, child.

"My parents were missionaries to Latin American countries and the Caribbean for 16 years before they had my brother and me. Then after they had us, of course, they continued to follow a Godly path. My family attended a very small Pentecostal church, and we went there from the time I was born until I was around 8-9 years old. Those were special times for me. The church was upstairs in a barn, out in the middle of nowhere, and there weren't even pews or cushioned chairs! I remember as a small child sitting in hard, folding chairs patiently waiting for the service to end (as any small child would, right?)."

"I have great memories of going to tent revivals when I was young. My brother and I would sit in the sawdust on the ground and play while singing endured, but when preaching started and the Word was being taught, we would sit beside each other on hard, wooden, bench-like pews, covered in quilts because most of the time they would have the revivals in the Fall, and they would carry on late into the night, sometimes until two and three in the morning! Those were good days…"

When Hannah became a teenager, she began to study other languages. "I've always been interested in different languages, cultures and religions. Even variant accents of English fascinate me. When I was a teenager, I began to study different widely-spoken languages, and Arabic happened to be one of those. The Arabic language and culture of Islam were definitely some things that I found intriguing."

She started studying the Qur'an and was intrigued by what she discovered. "The poetic flow of the verses in Arabic captivated me, and I found myself being increasingly, little by little, dominated by this religion. I also found Muslims (generally) to be very welcoming, and they offered a sense of "belonging" to those that were genuinely interested in learning about their faith."

But why was she really looking? What was she hoping to find in this exploration of other religions? Hannah explains, "I was typically the type of person that understood the practical side of things, versus the spiritual, more in-depth parts. If I couldn't see it, smell it, or hear it, then it must not be so. Growing up in a Christian home, the idea of the Trinity made absolutely no sense to me whatsoever. How could God be three different persons, yet be One? That question alone baffled me for a very long time. Along with several life events in a seemingly downward spiral, and a perplexed mind, it was there that I really began my search. I'd accepted as fact that my life was supposed to be full of affliction, misery and be altogether unfulfilling. What a lie! Thank Jesus that His love is enduring, and while weeping may endure for the night, joy DOES come in the morning!"

So Many Questions

Hannah decided that a "works-oriented religion" would be much easier to attain than blind faith in a Savior whose ways are more mysterious and complex than our own. (Isaiah 55:9 declares that in the same way that the heavens are higher than the earth...so are God's ways higher than our ways!)

"Another thing that I feel pulled me so strongly toward Islam," Hannah says, "is that I loved the practicality of it, and how simple it was to 'learn and do.'"

Her check list was pretty simple. 1) Shahada - swear that there is only one God and Mohamed is the last and final prophet.
2) Salat - Pray five times a day at specific times based on the moon.
3) Zakat – Give to the poor. 4) Sawm – Fasting.
5) Hajj -Pilgrimage to Mecca.

"I did all of these except for the last one. I didn't stay in the religion long enough to get that one accomplished, thank God, although I was planning for it daily! I woke up every morning before dawn, performed the ritual washing, and I said my prayers. I would then go back to sleep until time for me to really wake up for my day. Most days I was in school. At the appropriate time, I would leave during class, explaining to my teacher that I needed to go pray. I went to the bathroom, did the ritual washing, and prostrated right in the hallway (or wherever I happened to be at the specified time of prayer). I dressed as any young Muslim woman would. I layered my clothes, covering my entire body except for my face, hands and feet. I wore the hijab (headscarf) daily. It defined who I was: a part of the Islamic community." As Hannah told me her story, a question quickly floated to the front of my mind. "How did your Christian family and friends react to this radical change? What did they do?"

"I'm not entirely sure that my Christian friends and family knew the extent I had gone to follow this religion. I know they had an idea that I was dabbling in other religions and diligently searching, but I don't think they understood how deeply involved I was in it. I lived a sort of double life. In my early days of practicing Islam, when I visited my family back in my hometown, I acted like a Christian. I even attended church at times. Then when I went back to where I was living in Wilmington, I lived the Muslim life again."

"This constant alternating between faiths and lifestyles had me in a world of confusion. It seemed to be a bottomless pit of mental torment. I lay in bed at night praying to Allah (the false god), asking that if he was the true god, that he would please give me a sign and make it clear. Needless to say, I never got the affirmation I was looking for."

"Still, I continued my search. This made life more difficult, as I was a wretched person, so very miserable. I was deeply depressed, and it seemed everyone else around me would notice that my emotions were stricken. The one person that I think it affected the most is my mom. I was more open with her than a lot of other people in my life. She knew the struggle that I was going through, and she knew exactly how complicated my life had become by exposing myself to false religion."

"It had gotten to the point that every time I visited her, we would get into a heated argument as to whether or not my beliefs were correct, or if hers were. I challenged her to the point of blatant disrespect and didn't even realize it. The enemy was undoubtedly at work causing discord in my family. While it hurt me to know that she was hurting, I still found myself wallowing in my own world of selfishness. Not caring about what others had to say about my new life change, I only knew that I had a newly-found passion and I loved it, completely blind to the fact that it was damaging nearly every part of my life."

The Valiant Rescue
Okay, now it's time to get to the good stuff! The part where Jesus rides in on His white horse and saves the day! "Tell us, how exactly did this go down? How did Jesus draw your heart back to His?"

"This is kind of cool. One week I was visiting my dad during the summer of 2011. I got into a car accident while there, and I ended up being stuck without a car for weeks. I was so upset because I had registered for my classes in Wilmington, and here I was, inevitably stuck in Pinehurst. If I didn't get a car soon, I wouldn't have the means to be back in class that fall. These several weeks felt like some of the worst weeks of my life. I did a lot of praying. Although I was calling out to the wrong god, I still believe that in our Father's grace and mercy He heard my cries, because He is near to the brokenhearted and the crushed in spirit. Little did I know, the Lord works all things together for our good, for those that are called according to His purpose [Romans 8:28]."

"One Sunday afternoon a friend sent me a text message. She asked if I wanted to come hang out with her and several other people that I hadn't seen in just as long. I was very reluctant, and quite frankly I didn't want to. I knew that if I went to spend time with them, with it being a Sunday, I would also be invited to go to church with them that evening. My friend kept insisting that I come hang out. I finally accepted her offer and went to visit. I felt so ill at ease, but very quickly she made me feel comfortable and relaxed. What I thought was going to be awkward was an altogether graceful experience. Although I no longer felt anxious about being there around my friends, I did, however, feel anxious about what time it was. I kept finding myself glancing at the clock. Time was flying, and I knew they would soon leave for church and try their best to make me tag along. As six o'clock quickly approached, I could feel the most gripping anxiety creeping up within me. What was I to do? I was a Muslim girl. Muslims do not actively participate in the worship of another god, let alone the worship of a human being."

"The Christian faith, which I was raised to live by, had become a blurred memory far into the depths of my mind. I was engrossed in a completely different mindset; I had an entirely different concept of who the Supreme was. We arrived at the church, and before we even got into the parking lot, I began bawling."

"Uncontrollable sobs were rising up from deep within. Not knowing what was going on, my friend looked at me with distinct bewilderment. I could only mutter, "I don't know what's wrong with me." All the while, I knew that something was taking place within my spirit and within my soul. I gathered myself together. With wobbly knees, I got out of the car and walked inside the church. Once inside the foyer of my church, I began to sob again. Huge tears welled up in my eyes, racing down my face. I darted to the bathroom before anyone could see me."

"I then gathered myself a second time. I proceeded to go into the sanctuary. This was one of the most awe-inspiring experiences that I've had in my walk with the Lord, and I haven't experienced anything like it since. Upon entering the sanctuary, I could sense the weighty presence of the Almighty. He was making Himself so evident to me with near-tangible affirmation. He knows exactly what we need, when we need it. He knew I needed to know with absolute certainty that He was the Truth. This particular night was talent night at my church. A lady and her son sang a song, 'Through the Fire,' by the Crabb Family, and for a third time I began weeping uncontrollably. At that moment, a Voice spoke to me. It said, "Go to the altar." This Voice was so prominent; it was undeniably the voice of our Father, Who was speaking to me. A second time He said, "Go to the altar." I battled within myself, "Should I go? I don't believe Jesus is God. I just can't do this." Once more, the Voice said to me, "Go to the altar." This time it was not a mere Spirit-to-heart communication. I had heard Him even more outstanding than the first two times. I heard Him audibly. At the sound of His voice, I'd finally surrendered and rushed to the front of the church. I'd made my life right with our Lord and Savior. There were old friends that met me there, praying and crying with me. It was a beautiful act of surrender. I felt as though a huge weight, a thick darkness had been lifted from me. I could feel it, physically."

"When we submit to the drawing of the Holy Spirit, He is sure to retrieve us from the deepest pit. His Word tells us in Job 22:21 that when we submit to Him, and when we're at peace with Him, good things will come to us. This is true from the very moment we accept Him into our lives and hearts. It is an immediate move on our behalf, that He would grant us 'good things,' such as peace, love and joy. He is so faithful to carry us into His rest. All we have to do is simply acknowledge that He is Who He says He is; that is our Salvation and our Hope."

Coming Home to His Love

Today, Hannah is an absolute fireball, burning for Jesus Christ! From the outside looking in, one would never know the dark journey her heart went on, through deception and the valley of the shadow of death. All you can see is a heart shining with the light of Heaven, so brilliantly overjoyed to have found her forever home in His arms.

"I think the biggest thing I've learned since straying away from Him and then coming back, is just what your question is inquiring about: His Love!" Hannah continues, "I used to have this idea that God was angry with me. I thought that the circumstances in my life were His way of punishing me, and that I'd done something very awful in my childhood to make Him not like me. But that is far from the truth! He doesn't only love us with an immeasurable amount of love, He truly LIKES us! He likes spending time with us, talking to us, teaching us. We were created to have a natural friendship with the Lover of our souls! Since coming back to Jesus, it has been a very long journey of changing my mindset to understand His ways and His attributes. I am learning, every day, that He has crazy love for us!! There is nothing, absolutely NOTHING that could separate us from the love that He has for us. We are His perfect masterpiece, created and being ever transformed into His image. We are the righteousness of God through Christ Jesus. He longs for only one thing; our hearts."

Girl On A Mission

"'God will turn your mess into a message.' I've heard this countless times since becoming a born again believer. I definitely believe it rings true. When you live through something that was once your passion, I don't think that passion ever leaves. I believe it's simply channeled in another way. What once held you bound, I think God eventually uses for good. My past in Islam undoubtedly has affected my passion to preach the Gospel to Muslims now. I was one of them. It hurts my heart to know that there are nearly 2 billion Muslims in the world that don't know the love of Christ. They don't know who He is and what He did for them. They don't know that there's a Father in Heaven that is yearning for their hearts. They don't know that He DIED, that they might live eternally."

I have to ask the question, "Does it scare you to think about how much hostility there is in the Muslim community toward Christians? And why do you still want to witness to them with so many threats and dangers that could possibly come against you?"

"It does make me anxious to think about the hostility in the Muslim world. However, I am not afraid. I know Who goes before me, and I know Who stands behind. The Lord does not send us onto the battlefield without first equipping us for the good work He has called us to. The Qur'an is very clear about killing infidels and those that become apostates in their eyes. It actually states, "Disbelief is worse than killing…" It is no secret that the Islamic world is full of hatred and contempt toward Christians. It is also stated in the Qur'an that fighting is "prescribed" to Muslims. This hate-filled way of life toward others makes me all the more eager to share the Love-filled Gospel with them! Greater is He that is in me than he that is in the world…We cannot live life afraid of what could happen. We should be beacons of hope to the world, attesting to He who lives in us! "For I fully expect and hope that I will never be ashamed, but that I will continue to be bold for Christ, as I have been in the past. And I trust that my life will bring honor to Christ, whether I live or die." [Philippians 1:20]"

God is Faithful!
If you have unsaved friends or family members, don't be discouraged! Continue praying for them, and watch as God does a miracle in their

lives!

Just think what might have happened if Hannah's friend hadn't invited her to church; listen to what God places in your heart to do, and be obedient! It might just change someone's life!

~*~

I Dream of China

Most people don't know this about me, but I've had a strong vision for the land of China since I was a little girl. I remember holding my grandpa's hand when I was 5 years old; looking up into his eyes, telling him that someday I would be a missionary to China. It's something that has never left me!

My grandfather, who was an unusual prophet, was called to the land of Tibet. He had the same heart and love for China and Tibet! The Lord gave him a vision and a promise that one day He would send him to that nation. But it wasn't until 47 years later, at the age of 70, that the Lord fulfilled His promise and sent my grandfather. He went against all odds. Doctors begged him not to go and his reply would always be, "I don't think you understand, I have a mandate from God." You see, my grandfather was very ill with Congestive Heart Failure, Diabetes, etc., but God kept him.

His story has always inspired me because he was truly a living testimony of God's faithfulness! It has encouraged me to keep holding on to the vision that the Lord breathed in my Spirit at the tender age of 5-years-old. Here I am 15 years later, and my vision for the land of China is stronger than ever. I have had so many words given to me that have only confirmed what has been in my heart all along. At times I tell people my desire to be a missionary to China and the common responses I get is, "Don't you know how dangerous it is?" or, "It's a communist, filthy nation. Definitely not a place I want to go." Well every time I hear that, my grandpa's words, "I have a mandate from God," enter my mind. What I've learned is that not everyone is going to see or understand the things that the Lord shows you, but I've had to continue to believe that God will be faithful to His word.

My destiny will unfold at the appointed time, and I trust in my God full-heartedly that He is setting things in motion and opening doors for me that no man can shut. I believe full-heartedly that I will see the land of

China. I will have favor and be able to go into places that most people would have thought impossible to get into.

I share all this to encourage you with this: Maybe God has given you a dream that you have yet to see come to pass. Maybe you've been waiting for years, or maybe you even doubt if your vision really is from God. Do you ever feel weary in your season of waiting? I know I do at times. But there's a scripture that has become one of my all-time favorites that I want YOU to hold on to. Habakkuk 2:2-3 says: "Then the Lord answered me and said: Write the vision and make it plain on tablets. That he may run who reads it. For the vision is yet for an appointed time; but at the end it will speak and it will not lie. Though it tarries, wait for it. Because it WILL surely come. It will NOT tarry."

WOW, what a powerful promise from our Lord! Sisters, your vision is for an APPOINTED time, and it will not be late! God has placed whatever you're dreaming for in your heart for a purpose and reason. Even if people think you're crazy, don't let that stop you from holding on to your dream! Run with it! Like Habakkuk says, write it down. I encourage you ladies, to do that and remind the Lord of what He has promised. It's not that He needs a reminder, but God likes it when we hold Him accountable to His word and judge Him faithful.

Believe for what most people would think is impossible! Dream big because nothing is too hard for our God to accomplish! Walk by faith, but most importantly walk in obedience. It's through our faithfulness that His promises will come to pass.

Continue to have an unmovable faith, and TRUST that the Lord is going to accomplish everything He said He would in your life. He will not fail you! In fact, He will surpass all your expectations!

Love and Prayers,
Kenya-Nicole

~*~

Joy in the Journey

I believe that every dream has a journey. The journey for some is hard and even treacherous. The journey is an adventure. I don't know about you, but I love a good adventure! I love the challenges that accompany it.

There is something in me that enjoys a good dare. The world tells me I cannot see my dreams come true, but something inside me yells back, "Really? Watch me prove you wrong!" Sometimes the adventure is not so much fun and the journey is not so amazing. We see this beautiful dream that we want to come to pass, but we do not want to struggle or go through the process to see the dream come true.

Some of us, like my friend Kristin, may want to become a famous horse reiner, but we do not want to endure the pain of practicing endless hours with sore thighs. Maybe you want to find a cure for Cancer but you are failing at Science, and you do not want to spend your time studying instead of talking on the phone. There is a price to pay if we are to see our dreams come true. How bad do we want them? How much passion really lies inside of us for our dreams?

Joseph was a dreamer. He literally had some amazing dreams that God had given him. He was very passionate about his dreams and believed that God would bring them to pass. In the midst of his dreaming, he was thrown into a pit by his brothers. Then to make things even better, they sold him into slavery! He probably was very confused and hurt. Why would God give him dreams and visions but then allow him to be thrown into slavery?

Joseph continued to trust God. He found favor in the sight of Potiphar who was Pharaoh's main officer. Joseph was promoted as overseer, and life became better for him. One day Potiphar's wife noticed how attractive Joseph was. She eventually told him to sleep with her and he refused. He told her, "Look, with me here, my master doesn't give second thought to anything that goes on here – he's put me in charge of everything he owns. He treats me as an equal. The only thing he hasn't turned over to me is you. You're his wife, after all! How could I violate his trust and sin against God? (Genesis 39:8-9, MSG)"

Joseph knew that by refusing her he could lose his position and become a slave again. He was falsely accused by her and was then thrown into another pit – an Egyptian prison. He was there for quite a while according to scripture. His faith was truly tested. God had placed Joseph in that jail for a reason - he was preparing him to lead Egypt. He had to hold onto what God had spoken to him before he came to Egypt. He did not realize that God was about to take him from the pit to the palace. He had to endure that season of imprisonment first, and wait on God to bring him out. Joseph had to choose not to become bitter with the process.

While being imprisoned, God gave Him favor with the head jailer, and he was placed over all the prisoners. While in prison, he began to use the gift God had given him to interpret dreams. He interpreted the dreams of the other prisoners and eventually his gift brought him before the King. He was asked to interpret the dreams that were troubling the King, and after doing so, was made the head of Egypt. God exalted Joseph when he was ready, and when the nation needed him the most. The dreams that God had given him came to pass, and the joy was overwhelming after all the pain he had endured.

What prison or pit do you feel like you are in right now? Are you holding onto the dreams that God has given you? Are you willing to be found faithful where you are at?
God placed Joseph in that prison to build character in him. In that prison He learned how to trust God completely. He continued to use the gifts that God had given him, even in his pit.

There is something on the inside of you that God wants you to use in this season! Do you enjoy singing? Worship the Lord through this rough season. Worship gets our minds off ourselves and allows God to give us His perspective. We must have the right attitude in the journey before our dreams can come to pass.

Dream big and beautiful, but also embrace the journey. More importantly, embrace Jesus in the journey. There is a joy you will find as you seek God and praise Him in the midst of your process. The process prepares you for the position God is leading you into. Maybe you are dreaming of getting married someday and you feel like singleness is really dragging you down. Embrace this season! God is preparing your heart to be the woman of some man's dreams.

If we cannot be content in the journey, we are not ready for the destination! I have witnessed this in my own life. I have come so much closer to my King in this process. It has been very hard, but I have seen my pit become a palace as I embrace Jesus and bless those around me. He has been using the gifts He has placed inside me to help others and bring joy in this season.

He is preparing me for the days ahead, and when I realize that, it brings me so much comfort and joy. So let God satisfy your heart in this season of waiting, and trust.

He is the Lover of your soul! He is calling you to come closer to Him, and in the struggle He is your strength. Allow him to use the gifts inside you to bring joy to you and to others in the process. There are many things He wants to show you in this journey. Walk with Him and watch your dreams come true!

~Nellie Martin

~*~

PART 5: PRINCESS, DON'T FORGET...

Thoughts are always arguing and fighting for the space inside our heads. So what should we be filling it with? Everything pure, lovely, admirable, praise-worthy, true, and princess-y!

Don't forget these simple truths. Write them on sticky notes, Tweet them, post 'em on your bathroom mirror, or inside your locker at school. Let truth dig down deep in your soul! These are some of our favorite Tweets from our account @FoReVeR_ShineOn Follow us for daily encouragement!

~*~

They say beauty comes from clothes, cosmetics & instagram filters. The King says it comes from beholding His beauty & knowing His heart.

God doesn't measure success by numbers, crowds, or applause. He measures a heart by how big she loved.

Being single is not a sickness. It's a season: a beautiful, sweet, exciting one! Embrace it.

"Don't worry. Like seriously. I've got this." -Jesus

I am: Blessed. Chosen. Adopted. Redeemed. Forgiven. Loved Forever. #RoyaltyIsMyReality

"Turn my eyes away from worthless things; preserve my life according to Your word." Psalm 119:37

Sister, you are SO loved. Your Heavenly Father rejoices over you. Jesus sings songs over you. You are His great delight & precious daughter!

Skin is temporary. Hearts are forever. Sometimes we need to put away the lipstick, turn away from the mirror & return to what truly matters.

Your dreams are not random. God has placed unique dream seeds inside of You, that He desires to water and bring to life to touch this earth!

God's answer is never "Try harder." It's always "Fall into my arms, and rest in My love."

Princess, you have been created, chosen, and commissioned by Heaven to go change this world!

"You're insecure, don't know what for, you've been redeemed and loved by the Lord!" #WhatMakesYouBeautiful #Remix #If1DLovedJC #DayDreamin

Why are we obsessing over boy bands, thigh gaps & TV shows, when Jesus has called us to reach the broken and burn for Him? #RealityCheck

The Lord's Truth {His Word} always trumps our feelings. Tell your emotions to line up w His Word. Don't allow them to rule. #TruthTrumpsAll

You don't have to have it all figured out, in order to move forward. #FaithFirst #StepOutToFindOut #CliffJumping

Pure. Lovely. Nobel. Virtuous. Delightful. Of Good Report. Got these gems going on in your brain? Princess, fix your mind on these things!

"Indeed, the very hairs of your head are all numbered. Don't be afraid; you are worth more than many sparrows." Luke 12:7 #SoValuable

And sometimes, the phone has to simply be turned off. Return to reality. Your value does not depend on social media notifications.

You must know that today you are lovely. Today you are bold. Today you are free. Today you are Jesus' treasure & the apple of His eye!

#NeverForget that the Captain of the Angel Armies is on YOUR side. The God who breathed out the stars is for you, not against you.

Your uniqueness is adorable in God's eyes. He totally delights in you! You make Him smile. You're His Princess. His Daughter. His lovely one.

You are NOT a worrier. You ARE a warrior.

Your uniqueness is a daily reminder of how much God adores you, and how much thought and energy He spent creating you!

The things you are passionate about are not random. They were planted there for a purpose. #PassionAndPurpose

Touch a little girl, and you touch the women of tomorrow. Change a little girl, and you change the world.

Mirror, mirror on the wall you don't know what you're talking about at all.

Cinderella was a princess far before she ever reached the palace. She lived each day with humility and kindness.

Every day we have the choice to either align our thoughts with God's perfect truth, or empower the enemy by believing his lies. #ChooseTruth

We cannot afford to think differently about ourselves than God does. We must see ourselves through His eyes. Forgiven. Loved. Royalty.

Comparison is joy's greatest thief. Don't waste another day "wishing" it away. Your life is a gift. Be you. Fully, freely, and completely.

Jesus served with the heart of a King. And He rules with the heart of a servant. #HumilityIsRoyalty

Love doesn't mean you're changing the world all at once. Love is stopping for the person right in front of you and changing their world.

"For the Lord will give grace and glory: no good thing will he withhold from them that walk uprightly." Psalm 84:11

Reality Check: You have an address etched into a street of gold, in Heaven! You are not a citizen of this world. You're just passing through.

There's freedom in abandonment, and relief in letting go. When tight, white knuckles release, God is free to move. #SurrenderIntoHisHands

Rapunzel, Rapunzel, you don't need to let down your hair OR your standards. Don't make it easy. Your prince will find a way to climb UP there!

Don't let discouragement leave you feeling like a doormat. It's a worthwhile fight. Press on and press in. Victory is yours.

Dreamer, this life is so short. God placed that dream inside you for a purpose. All of heaven is cheering you on. Go for it. #Unstoppable

#DearFutureHusband There's a reason I'm single today... Because I love you with my whole heart & won't settle for anything less than you!

Dreamer, it doesn't matter how slow you go or how long it takes. Just as long as you keep going and refuse to quit! #Unstoppable

Alone. Ugly. Unloved = MAJOR LIES. Beautiful. Confident. Secure in Christ. Radically loved.
Heiress of the King of Kings = MAJOR TRUTH.

Little girls with {BIG} dreams become women with {CLEAR, UNSTOPPABLE & WORLD CHANGING} vision!

Seize that loveliness. It has always been yours. You were made in the image of God. You have greatness inside of you. You sparkle for Him.

God's love is so much better than Starbucks. He desires to pour His toasty love into our hearts like warm coffee bubbling in a mug.

Always choose to speak life, no matter what you feel. Feelings fade, but the Word of the Lord stands forever. Stand on His truth today!

You were not created to be a repeat of someone else. He wanted to do a NEW thing on this earth, and thus came = you! Own your uniqueness! :)

Your dreams reflect a unique part of God's heart. Don't ignore them. You've been called to manifest that part of His character on the earth!

Waiting to hear from God about what He wants you to do with your life? Maybe He's waiting to hear from you about the dream in your heart!

Singleness isn't a curse. It's a sweet season to lean into the heart of our Savior, and experience the most perfect love in the Universe.

Perhaps the thing that you are waiting for isn't even the ultimate prize. Maybe the true treasure is what you are gaining in the process.

There is a reason for the season that you're in. There's a purpose for the waiting. Trust that it is good and perfect. God holds your days!

"One man's overlooked blessing is another man's happily ever after." -Kenya-Nicole

You don't need a promotion to feel better about yourself. Your Daddy is the King & CEO of the Universe. That's as high up as you can go!

Be who you want to be because that's actually who you were created to be. That's WHY you want to be it. #BeTheRealYou

Royalty doesn't focus on the platform, the power, or the sparkly stage lights. Royalty only sees {and loves} the hurting people.

Don't ignore your dreams. Your dream just might save a life. If Joseph would have abandoned his dreams, thousands of people would have died.

Your dreams are not just for you. Someone out there desperately needs your gift, whatever it is that you can so easily give. It's unique.

Beautiful isn't a physical status you are struggling to attain. Beautiful is already your identity. Beautiful is your name.

Dreams are quiet reminders that we were made for more. It's the gentle nudge within our hearts to pursue what God has created us to do & be.

Everything we are craves Heaven. We are so thirsty for God! When we chase after Him, He fills us up & our appetite for this world grows dull.

She wasn't afraid to shine. With glitter dust on her fingertips, a song in her heart, & a crown on her head, she set out to change the world.

Sparkle with the heavenly splendor which God has bestowed upon you. You are His princess. You shine like stars in the universe! #ShineOn

Humility. It is our secret weapon. Patience. It is our strength. Kindness. It is our sword. Quiet & steady trust in God wins wars.

You are unique and uniquely loved. There is no one on this universe who touches & moves God's heart in the same exact way you do. Be you.

You don't need dozens of thumbs up on your selfies, your face on the cover of a magazine, or a boyfriend to give you a sense of self-worth.

You ARE beautiful. You are the girl *One Direction* sings their love songs about...they just don't know it yet. ;)

Everything you have dreamed about who you could be is actually who U were made to be! Princess. Brave. Forever adored by the King of Kings.

"For the Lord sees not as man sees; for man looks on the outward appearance, but the Lord looks on the heart." 1 Samuel 1:16

1 Samuel 16 has great relationship advice. Don't fall for the first 7 attractive guys that come along...wait for the one GOD has chosen!

God sees more than we do. Guard your heart. Don't give it away too soon. Wait for your David. He will be a ruddy, handsome, Godly warrior! ;)

Why are we so worried about what other people think? Live like nobody is watching. Cause they're not. They're checking their phones. Seriously.

If we had a world full of women who cared for & nurtured others more than we obsess over our own mirrors & lives...this world would change.

You are the highest and greatest treasure in the King's heart. He sings a song of celebration over you every day! <3

"Do not despise these small beginnings, for the LORD rejoices to see the work begin." -Zechariah 4:12 #DreamBig #StartSmall

Whoever you watch, listen to & read is who you become. Fill your mind & heart with messages of truth. Surround yourself with women of virtue.

Don't put yourself in a box. The God Almighty who created you in His image doesn't have any boxes! So why should you? #LiveFree #InHisImage

If you dared to discover who God has truly created you to be, you'll never want to be anyone else! #GodsWord #DigIn #BeTheYouHeMadeYouToBe

God doesn't create mistakes. Don't criticize the stunning piece of artwork that you are!

Job Description of a Princess: To see broken hearts healed, captives set free, prison doors flying open & darkness overcome by His Light.

Job Description of a Princess: "Speak up for those who cannot speak for themselves, for the rights of all who are destitute." Prov 31:8

"Our society is too obsessed with numbers...rates, weight, followers, likes, just stop. You only need one, and that's God." -Julia Walton

If you want a man built by God & not by this culture, you're going to have to wait for it. Strong skyscrapers take longer to build. #WorthIt

God's love is inexhaustible. You can never exaggerate it. Attempting to fathom His love is like trying to scoop up the ocean with a tea cup!

Don't go around kissing frogs. It won't turn him into a prince. But it may turn YOU into a frog! :0 #HighStandards

"For He alone satisfies the longing soul, and fills the hungry soul with goodness." Psalm 107:9 Can't find it anywhere else. Only in Jesus!

~*~

Made in the USA
Lexington, KY
30 April 2016